Adela Elizabeth Orpen

**Perfection City**

Adela Elizabeth Orpen

**Perfection City**

ISBN/EAN: 9783742897060

Manufactured in Europe, USA, Canada, Australia, Japa

Cover: Foto ©Lupo / pixelio.de

Manufactured and distributed by brebook publishing software (www.brebook.com)

Adela Elizabeth Orpen

**Perfection City**

# PERFECTION CITY

BY

MRS. ORPEN

AUTHOR OF MARGARETA COLBERG, MR. ADOLF,
THE CHRONICLES OF THE SID, ETC.

NEW YORK
D. APPLETON AND COMPANY
1897

# CONTENTS.

| CHAPTER | PAGE |
|---|---|
| I.—Home-coming of the bride | 1 |
| II.—Uncle David | 11 |
| III.—Sister Mary Winkle | 21 |
| IV.—Madame Morozoff-Smith | 27 |
| V.—Corn planting | 43 |
| VI.—Non-resistance | 54 |
| VII.—Willette | 66 |
| VIII.—Mr. Perseus | 84 |
| IX.—First lessons | 101 |
| X.—Practical communism | 111 |
| XI.—A chance meeting | 125 |
| XII.—The prairie fire | 141 |
| XIII.—The rescue | 156 |
| XIV.—Cotterell "wanted" | 170 |
| XV.—In quest of news | 185 |
| XVI.—Horse thieves | 204 |
| XVII.—A life at stake | 219 |
| XVIII.—Lynch law | 237 |
| XIX.—Olive missing | 251 |
| XX.—Madame's sympathy | 263 |
| XXI.—The message | 277 |
| XXII.—Olive's second home-coming | 293 |
| XXIII.—Conclusion | 305 |

# PERFECTION CITY.

## CHAPTER I.

### HOME-COMING OF THE BRIDE.

"This road isn't called Perfection Road, is it?" she asked jerkily, as she held tight hold of the edge of the waggon to prevent herself from being pitched head foremost off the seat. She would have laid her head against her companion's shoulder only that it was square and hard, and she was afraid of getting her temple "stove in," as the sailors say, by the terrific bumps caused by the wheels going over a big stone or down into a deep rut. She was a bride, and he was bringing her to their new home on the Kansas Prairie.

"My poor little pet," he said tenderly, "it is very rough here. We are going down into Cotton Wood Creek, and these stones were cast up by the last freshet which pretty well washed the road away."

They plunged headlong into the muddy waters of the Creek, and the little bride would have felt frightened only that "he" was by her side, for the waggon creaked and groaned with the strain, and the horses snorted uneasily, feeling their way carefully through the rushing torrent. The Creek was safely passed, and they slowly toiled up the long hill out of the bottom-lands, and pulled up when once more on the high prairie.

"There is our home, dearie," he said, pointing with his whip to some scattered houses a couple of miles away. And being a bridegroom he kissed her.

"So that is Perfection City, is it?" said she, shading her eyes with her hand, for the afternoon sun sent level rays into her face. "You know, Ezra, it is such a funny name, I always feel inclined to laugh when I say it. And how I shall ever dare to put it at the top of my letters as a real address when I write to the girls at the College at Smyrna, is more than I know."

"Then don't write it," replied Ezra, a trifle sternly. "It will hurt our feelings very much if you laugh at it. You know it means a great deal to all of us."

"Then I'll never laugh at it," said the little bride.

"Which is our house?" she asked a moment later.

"The one half way up the slope."

"Oh, that is nice. I like looking down across things. I shouldn't like to live in a valley and always have to look up, you know."

"The large building is the Academy," said Ezra. "That is where we hold our meetings and gather together for all the best purposes of our little community-life."

"Is it there that Madame Morozoff-Smith lives?" asked his wife.

"Her house is the one just opposite."

"Oh, that big one! It is quite the largest in the village—the City, I mean."

Ezra did not make any reply to this remark. He had never realised that Madame's house was indeed the largest in their Community, and now he felt vexed that this fact should have been the first his wife noted.

A small boy with shining black face and shining white teeth, along with a yellow puppy, welcomed them.

"This is Napoleon Pompey," said Ezra, with much decorum presenting the small darkie who grinned and bobbed his head. "And this is Diana," pointing to the puppy that had come up to the bars along with the negro. Diana jumped upon her new mistress and left two black dust marks on her dress. Dust is black in London and on the western prairie, nowhere else.

"Oh, you dirty dog," said the little bride, who was a very natty body.

"You'll have to get used to dirt in all degrees out here, Ollie," said her husband as he led her to the door. She looked like a little girl as she stood beside him, for he was tall and angular and long of leg. A sloping plank with battens nailed across it led to the door, there were no steps. As the pair entered, Napoleon Pompey and Diana took the horses and waggon to the stable and began respectively to unharness and worry them.

"What a dear little house! It is just like a toy! And do look at the saws hanging on the walls beside the covers of the pots! Oh, won't it be so nice and free living here! I shall feel like an explorer in a far country. And how funny to have nail kegs for seats, and oh, you dear old darling!"

Olive jumped up and kissed her big husband.

"Things are rough now, dearie," he said with infinite tenderness, looking at her with loving admiration, "but by and by we shall have everything very nice."

"But I think it is just as nice as it can be now."

"This is our room," said he, opening a door to the right.

"Why, if you haven't gone and got a rocking-chair!" exclaimed Olive, glancing around the small apartment.

"I made it for you myself in spare time," answered Ezra, pleased that she had noticed the chair the first thing: he had often wondered, when working at that rocking-chair, whether she would be pleased with it. "You see," he continued, "we have to work only five days a week for the Community. All the rest of our time is at our own disposal, and by and by, when we are flourishing, four days for the Community will suffice."

"Do you like working for other people and not being paid?" asked Olive.

"I do not consider it as working for other people without pay," replied her husband, with some quickness. "We each work for the general good, and if I happen to plant corn that someone else will eat, then some other member of the Community raises potatoes that I shall eat."

"There, there, don't be cross," said the little wife, noting the flush that had risen to his brow as he spoke. "I am sure it is nice, and I shall like it when I understand it all. At any rate we shall be very happy whatever happens, and I like my dear little house, and please, I am very thirsty, can I have a drink?"

He brought her some water in a tin dipper with a long handle, and she did not make a face, but drank the water gratefully. She determined in her own mind, however, to have a glass tumbler the very next day, but she was new to the prairie, and she did not get the tumbler the next day, nor the next week, nor for many, many long months.

"What time are we to have breakfast?" she asked, when taking over the household from Napoleon Pompey and Diana, who had run the establishment while her husband had been to fetch her from Ohio.

"Yo' kin eat when yo' like," said Napoleon Pompey, desiring to be all that was polite to his new mistress.

"But I want to know what time you have breakfast?" repeated Olive with persistence.

"We uns got ter be hout on der lan' ploughin' afore sun-up," said Napoleon Pompey concisely.

"Dear me! Why, that is before six o'clock!" exclaimed Olive.

"I calkerlate," said Napoleon Pompey affably.

Ezra did not want Olive to think she was bound to get up and prepare the working-man's breakfast.

"You are not used to that sort of hard work, dearie. We can do very well with cold corn-bread."

"Of all things the most stoggy and hopelessly uninviting," interrupted his wife. "No, Ezra, I won't have any of the people out here think I am a little fool that can't do any useful work. I have my pride as well as other folks. I shall cook your breakfast to-morrow and every day afterwards, and I shall cook it well, see if I don't."

"I am sure of that," said her husband with the confidence of a bridegroom.

The house of which the young bride had just taken possession was by no means an ordinary prairie house. Far from it. It had pretensions to comfort which the true prairie house should never possess, and it lacked the few elements of picturesqueness with which the genuine article is sometimes endowed. The plan on which it was built was of the simplest—the same that children adopt in building their doll's houses—four sides and a sloping roof, all of wood from top to bottom. It was not a log-house, which has a few broken lines to rest the eye of the beholder and present possibilities to the artist, it was a frame house, that is, the straightest, stiffest, squarest, most hopelessly unpicturesque object that it is possible to imagine, and to make matters worse it was painted a glaring white from eave to foundation. There was not a broken line or a broken tint anywhere to refresh the eye, and it stood on the high prairie, as if hurled into a glaring world by a Titan's hand.

The prairie is fertile, and in the eye of a farmer may possess the beauty of usefulness, but otherwise it is hideous. The long rolling billows of grass present no character, while the trees are confined to the river valleys where they find refuge from prairie fires, and can therefore lead a sufficiently undisturbed existence to reach quite a respectable height. A couple of small locust trees, not three feet high, were all that did duty as shade-giving plants near Olive's house, which accordingly faced the world and its storms entirely on its own individual merits. Judged by prairie standard the house was "tip-top." It possessed no less than four rooms, while the regular settler's cabin was wont to indulge in only a single comprehensive apartment, which was kitchen, parlour and bed-room all in one. The two lower rooms were the kitchen, which was fairly large, and a smaller one off it, reserved for the private use of the young wife. The kitchen looked like a ship's cabin, only that it had more light than usually penetrates into a ship's cabin. In fact it was very light, for there were two large windows, one to the north and one to the south, geometrically opposite each other. These two windows, so exactly facing each other, were fairly typical of the house itself, which was the embodiment of mathematical accuracy. The building was placed exactly east and west, as if it had been a carefully oriented church. There was a door on the south side, exactly in the middle, and a window on either side of the door, placed accurately in the centre of the space left between the side of the door and the end of the house. Over these two windows were two others exactly one half their size, giving light to the loft, and exactly in the centre of the roof-ridge was a black stove-pipe.

The average prairie man is a genius in the way of doing without things. He can live in a house of the smallest dimensions, containing the minimum of utensils. In fact, his idea of a house is that it should be a miner's tent solidified into substantiality. The miner in a newly-prospected gold-field is a person who spends his days in a hole, and has no belongings but the clothes on his back and the shovel in his hand. He lives on his expectations. The regular prairie settler, would arrive in the spring, camp in his waggon, stick grains of corn under the sod, and think himself lucky if he could raise both the corn and a log-hut, fourteen by twelve feet, before the cold weather set in. Those who have passed through such a severe school prune down their requirements. Therefore the house to which Ezra Weston brought his little bride was rightly considered to be a model of luxury, or in prairie phraseology to be " powerful full o' truck."

The kitchen certainly was full. The stove, black and business-like, stood near the partition wall, and on it rested a couple of huge iron pots with covers. Chairs there were none, as Olive had remarked, but boxes and nail-kegs did as well and were useful in holding things. There was a large wooden table, very strongly made, on one side, and a set of shelves in one corner. The walls and ceiling, which were of wood closely jointed, added to the ship-like appearance of the room, but the presence of two large saws and a horse-collar which hung above them made a considerable deduction from the nautical character of the apartment.

This model dwelling stood in the midst of a large tract of fenced-in land. Part of this was already under cultivation and showed a dark purple surface to the heavens, betokening newly turned up prairie sod full of the natural plant foods stored there for thousands of ages. These were now about to be recklessly used up by the ordinary system of prairie farming, which consisted of taking everything out of the land and of putting nothing back into it. A sort of road, that is to say a beaten track with deep channels on either side, led from the house to the bars, which did duty as gate to the premises. These bars were precisely what the name implies, bars of wood lying on supports made for them between posts, and they were simply let down whenever horses or other animals had to pass in or out, and were climbed over by active children too lazy to let them down or rather, perhaps, too lazy to put them up again.

On one side of the bars stretching out at an angle was an orchard just planted with trees that probably would be worth having twenty years hence, and further away was another field consisting simply of fenced-in prairie grass. The fields, and indeed everything else, were square, and every fence that did not run north and south, ran east and west. The whole place seemed under a despotism of compass and measuring chain. Indeed, the prairie itself was under the same iron rule: and by the authorities had been plotted out into squares of a mile each way called "sections," of which persons could buy of the Government quarter sections or multiples of a quarter section at a low rate. Fortunately for humanity this conspiracy to turn the world into a surveyor's map was to some extent defeated by the rivers and streams, which ran as Heaven and the water-sheds decreed, and not as the officials at Washington desired. This fact, and this alone, has in some measure saved the prairie from the awful fate of mathematical damnation.

## CHAPTER II.

### UNCLE DAVID.

Mrs. Weston was tired and sat down in her rocking-chair to rest. Her day's work was fairly over. The breakfast had been ready punctually at half past five, and it was well-cooked, as she had boasted it would be—corn-bread smoking hot, fried chicken, potatoes, flap-jacks and molasses—a meal for a king, to say nothing of a working-man and his negro help. Ezra and Napoleon Pompey had partaken heartily, especially the latter, for he had been living on underdone hoe-cake and cold pork. Then they had gone off to the ploughing, while Olive had bustled around and got forward with her house-work. At eleven o'clock she had run up the towel against the shady side of the house, a signal easily seen from the distant field, and signifying that dinner was ready. They had come home, men and horses thoroughly hungry and ready for food and rest. Ezra lay on the kitchen floor and talked to her while she washed up the dishes. And now it was three o'clock, and all the work was done. She thought she would read a little. She had several books with her that she had been looking forward to reading. So she took up one of them and seated herself comfortably in the rocking-chair. The door was open and a warm air came in from the south along with the gleaming sunshine. Diana lay across the door-way, but kept one eye open, so as to see when the black hen came near enough to have a spring at her with any chance of grabbing a mouthful of tail-feathers. Olive's eyes rested very little on the book, but much on the view outside. It looked pleasant enough in the bright May sunshine. The long brown patch of the garden showed a few methodical green lines that spoke of vegetables beginning to sprout. The meadow of blue grass just beyond was likewise by its hue showing the on-coming of the warm spring weather, and yet again further off, on the other side of the meadow, lay the vast field which her husband was ploughing. Once in every half hour she could see him turn at the head-land, and noted how seldom he seemed to stop and rest. Napoleon Pompey was riding the off leader, and from that distance they seemed little insects gently crawling backwards and forwards across the land. Pleasant it looked too and by no means hard work. Olive determined to go out to the field one day soon and watch the process from a nearer point of view; she might indeed herself hold the plough-handles, it looked easy, she would ask Ezra to let her, she would like to learn to do all sorts of work so as to be very useful, she would—confused images swept slowly over her mind, she leaned back her pretty little head and slept in her chair.

She awoke with a start. A large square figure stood in the doorway, blocking out the sunshine, and Diana, with the insane friendliness of a puppy, was trying to clamber up one of his legs.

"Well, little gal, I reckon you're 'most tired out, ain't you?" said the big man, coming straight into the room.

Mrs. Weston rose to her utmost height of five feet two inches, and tried to be dignified.

"Do you wish to see my husband?" she inquired stiffly.

"No, I don't want to see Ezry. I come to talk to you a spell, and see you."

"You are very kind I'm sure," returned the little lady icily, but the stranger did not seem one whit abashed. He took a nail-keg and sat down on it and looked about him. "Wal, now," he remarked, nodding his head, "Ezry is real downright handy. He's gone and got your house fine and fixed up, ain't he now?"

"It is extremely comfortable, Mr.—ah—I don't think you mentioned your name," said Mrs. Weston, with a snap of her black eyes. She didn't at all relish the free and easy way in which this man spoke of her husband.

"Do tell!" exclaimed the stranger with vast cordiality. "An' you didn't know who I was. Why, I'm

Uncle David. I guessed everybody 'ud know me. There ain't nobody else so big and awkward looking 'bout here on this prairie as me. Why, there was a man over to Perfection City yesterday, he come from beyond Cotton Wood Creek, and he said he calculated I'd be powerful useful on washing days, 'cause if they tied the clothes-line to me I'd do instead of a pole, an' timber is mighty scarce anyhow."

Uncle David gave a long loud laugh that set Diana into an ecstasy of delight, and was of itself so joyous that, after a moment, Olive also joined in with a merry titter. She had often heard her husband speak of Uncle David, as being one of the kindest and most simple-hearted of men. Her frigid manner melted rapidly and completely.

"Wal, now," began Uncle David again, after his merriment had subsided, "how do you like our name?"

"Your name," repeated Olive considerably puzzled.

"No, our name, the name of the Community, Perfection City. Do you like it?"

"I don't think I do," replied she.

"Jes' so," broke in Uncle David, apparently much pleased with this answer. "I knew you wouldn't. Nobody does."

"Why did you call it such a name—such a horrid name—and if nobody likes it, what is the use?"

"There now, that's what they all say, until I talk

to 'em," said Uncle David. "You see I gave the name to the place."

"Oh, it was your choice!" said Olive.

"When we came here, Niece and I, there wasn't no town nor nothing, it was just open prairie. Ezry he come along too with us, and the Carpenters, and Mrs. Ruby, and the Wrights."

"You leave out Madame Morozoff-Smith," interrupted Olive.

"I thought you knew. Why, Madame, she's Niece. She ain't my real niece, she wasn't born in my family, but she's niece by adoption, and I hold she's more to me than half the nieces I ever seen. I ain't cute like most of the folks here, an' there wasn't no use in having me at Perfection City. I can't do nothing. I can't compose papers like Brother Wright. So I was studyin' to see some way for me to come with 'em. It would ha' broke my heart to be left behind. Madame, she come to me, an' says she: 'You'll be my uncle. I want an uncle very much, and I'll love you dearly.' An' so I was. I call it the greatest honour of my life when Madame made me her uncle, and added my name to hers." Uncle David stooped and patted Diana's head thoughtfully.

"When did you think of the name?" said Olive with a view to bringing him back to the point.

"Yes, jes' so, that's 'xactly what I was comin' to. You see, when Ezry fust come here with us he wasn't quite clear in his mind 'bout joinin' in with us, leastways not to be one of the Community for his whole mortal life. It's a serious step to take, and he was a-doubtin' in his mind, leastways till Madame she talked to him for a spell. He wasn't sure fust if he'd got a call to community-life. He knowed it was the best, of course, and the true life: he knowed all that right enough, but he didn't feel sure of himself as bein' fit to found a city. It is a most responsible thing to be a founder. 'Taint everybody as is fit for it. Then Madame made it clear how she was a founder, an' she is the most wonderful woman ever lived in this world, an' she showed Ezry how it was his duty to help in this great work, an' when he saw that clear he was dreadful sot on it too. We was a-gettin' our houses up as spry as ever we could, and ole Wright he was a-buildin' th' Academy, then Ezry says: 'What's goin' to be our name?' It was jes' called Weddell's Gully, 'cause we bought from a man o' that name. So Ezry said: 'Let's call it something to signify our principles,' and one person said one name and one said another, then Wright said 'Let's call it Teleiopolis.'"

"Oh, that sounds very pretty," exclaimed Olive. "Why didn't you?"

"Wal, now, I said that's very pretty, jes' the same as you did. What does it mean, do you know?"

"No, I don't know. I suppose it is Greek for something."

"'Zactly so. It is Greek for something, and that something is Perfection City."

"It sounds nicer."

"Maybe so, but you look here. Are we Greeks?"

"No, of course not."

"Then why talk in Greek?"

"I don't know, except it is prettier."

"Do you suppose them old Greeks, when they went an' founded cities, they called 'em names out o' some other language they didn't understand, or did they called 'em good solid Greek names as any little boy 'ud know what they meant?" asked Uncle David with rising energy.

"I believe they called their cities by Greek names, in fact I know they did," said Olive, hastily reviewing her stock of history.

"An' why?" asked Uncle David.

"I don't know."

"Because they wasn't 'shamed o' their mother tongue like we are. That's why," said Uncle David, clapping his big hand on his knee.

"Oh indeed," said Olive.

"An' that's what I said, says I, 'We are 'Mericans, we are founding a new city that's goin' to be great things one day. We have our principles. Let's live up to them. We hain't shamed o' nothin'. Leastways not to my knowledge. We are goin' to be an example to these folks roun' here. We are goin' to show 'em how to live a better life nor they ever did before. An' how in thunder can we do that if we start by being 'shamed of our own mother tongue? We hain't

Greeks, we don't talk in Greek. This hain't Teleiopolis, this is Perfection City.' That is what I said to 'em."

"What did they say to that?" asked Olive, much interested in the rugged honesty of Uncle David.

"Wal, I don't know as they said anything much, on'y Ezry, he said he guessed he'd had his fust lesson, an' he come and shook hands an' said it certainly should be Perfection City, an' so it was."

"I shall think better of the name now," said Olive. "Only at first I was afraid of people laughing, people who didn't understand it, you see."

"Oh, people 'll laugh," said Uncle David. "People does a heap o' laughing in this world without makin' it one mite merrier for anybody. I like laughing myself. It's awful good an' satisfyin' to have a real square laugh, but t'aint that sort. Mos' folks' laugh hain't got no more fun in it than the laugh of a hoot-owl. I'd a heap sight rather have none at all. You ain't agoin' to mind that sort, I hope?" Uncle David spoke with a shade of anxiety in his manner.

"Oh no, I'm not thin-skinned," said Olive with a superior smile.

"Some folks is made that way. When they have found a tender spot in anybody they can't rest no how till they've stuck some sort o' pin into it."

"Tell me, does everything belong to everybody generally out here? It is so puzzling. This house, for instance, is it ours or yours or everybody's?" asked Olive.

"The land an' the horses an' the cattle an' waggons was mostly bought with community-money, that is Madame, she gave the money, she's rich you know, an' she's generous and always givin' to the Community, her whole heart is in it. But Ezry worked a heap on this house, he mostly built it all, an' it's his, an' t'other folks' houses are theirs. That's Brother Wright's over yonder, an' that's our house beside the 'Cademy, most everybody worked to get it up and fix it comfortable for Madame. Old Mrs. Ruby, she lives to herself in the log cabin we bought from Weddell, we had it moved there a purpose over from the Gully, 'cause she liked to live beside the spring so as to get her water handy. She had a little mite of money which we used in buyin' stock."

"So you do have some things as private property, just like ordinary people," observed Olive.

"Of course. It would not be any sort o' use to have everything in common, 'cause folks' notions don't always 'xactly suit. An' what we want is to have everybody free, so they can be perfectly happy here. We don't want to have no strife, an' no jealousy, an' no ill feeling one towards another. But there can't be community in all things. What sort o' use would it be for you an' me to have community o' boots an' shoes?" said Uncle David with a great laugh, sticking out his enormous foot towards where

Olive's dainty little slipper peeped from beneath her dress.

"Your shoes, my dear, wouldn't go on my two fingers, an' mine 'ud be big enough to make a tol'eble boat for you. There couldn't be community in shoes, so there ain't none. But with the lan' it's different. We all work that for the benefit of everybody, there ain't no strugglin' to be fust an' get ahead o' one another. We are all brothers at Perfection City."

Olive was full of excitement when Ezra came back at sun-down.

"Just fancy, I've had my first visitor," she said as she stood beside her husband while he was watering the horses.

"Who was it? Mrs. Ruby?"

"No, it was Uncle David," and she gave a merry little laugh.

"Well, and how did you like him?"

"I think he is just charming. He is just like a piece of granite or oak or something of that sort, not smooth or shiny on the outside, but solid and sound to the very core. Oh! I shall love Uncle David."

"That's right. He is a good man," said Ezra.

"And you know? he has made me understand about Perfection City. I shan't want to laugh at it any more, and I don't care if anybody else does. It was real brave of you showing your colours plain and sticking to them," said Olive with a skip and a clap of her little hands.

## CHAPTER III.

#### SISTER MARY WINKLE.

The very next morning just as she was washing her potatoes for dinner, another visitor called upon Olive, a visitor of whose sex she was for a moment or two in doubt. The visitor wore a large sunbonnet, a check blouse, and a pair of Zouave trowsers fastened in at the ankle.

"How do you do, Olive Weston?" said this person, in a deep serious voice. Olive, who had not seen her, started in surprise and dropped her potato into the basin.

"I am Mary. Winkle. That's my house over yonder."

"Oh, the Wrights'! Yes, to be sure. Come in and sit down," said Olive hospitably, although she felt considerable surprise at her visitor's appearance.

"You don't wear the reformed dress yet, I see," said Mary Winkle.

"No, I don't," acquiesced Olive.

"Shall you?"

"I don't know. I have not thought about it.

I suppose there is no regulation about what one wears on the prairie. There is no fashion here I suppose," said Olive politely.

"No, only the fashion of common sense."

"Do all the ladies dress that way, Miss Winkle?" inquired Olive.

"Only my daughter and myself."

"I beg your pardon, I should have said Mrs. Winkle," said Olive, in some confusion.

"No, you shouldn't," replied her visitor. "I am not Mrs. Winkle."

"I am afraid I am very stupid. Would you tell me then how I should address you. I don't understand."

"Address me as Mary Winkle, and my husband as John Wright."

Olive stared at her.

"Are you not Mrs. Wright then?"

"No, certainly not. I scorn the title. It is a symbol of subjection. I did not lose my identity when I chose to marry. I am the same Mary Winkle that I was before, and as such I desire to retain the name that I always possessed. Why should I take a new name simply because I am married?"

"It is usual," stammered Olive. "I shouldn't like not to be called Mrs. Weston. It is so confusing, you see."

"Mere custom and prejudice. Why should not your husband take your name, instead of its always being the wife who is absorbed?"

"I don't know, but I never heard of it before."

"Ah, that is one of the first changes that must be made when women get their rights," observed Mary Winkle.

"But I don't want the change one bit. I much prefer the old way."

"I dare say. Slaves often feel no want of freedom."

"I'm not a slave," said Olive, flushing angrily. "You cannot be in the least acquainted with my husband."

"Oh, I know your husband very well, an excellent man in many respects, but narrow in others; however, I referred to general slavery, to custom, not to any individual slavery in your case."

"I don't think there is any good in destroying customs, unless there is something better to be got in a new custom."

"Ah yes, no doubt it seems so to you; but there is inestimable gain in the mere protest against tyranny. Why, that's what we are all here for, to protest against everything and live a life of freedom."

"And freedom may as well begin here and now, and in its name I will wear long dresses and be called Mrs. Weston, because I prefer the older customs," said Olive with some archness.

"Yes, you may do as you like, but you will get heartily sick of those skirts, I can tell you."

Olive remembering sundry pretty dresses she had

in her trunk, was privately convinced she would not get sick of them.

"I haven't seen Madame yet," she said, "and I feel the greatest curiosity about her. She must be a remarkable woman by all accounts. Does she wear the same sort of dress as you do?"

"No, she doesn't, and it's a great pity, for her influence would be very great with the other women. I suppose you'll see her to-morrow evening. You'll come to the Academy, won't you?"

"Yes, certainly, if Ezra is going. I should like to go ever so much and see all my neighbours, but perhaps he will be too tired. He does work dreadfully hard, it seems to me."

"He ought to do a little brain-work. Wright says nothing rests one like brain-work. He's been doing a spell of that lately. He's been writing an essay on 'The Ultimate Perfection of Being.' He'll most likely read some of it to-morrow at the Academy."

"I shouldn't think essays would be much use in planting corn," said Olive rather tartly, remembering at what hour her husband had come from the harrowing.

"Wright and I, we don't believe in making a god of work. We have a much higher ideal of life than that. We don't want anything sordid in our lives, Wright and I. We haven't any sympathy with this restless striving to get on. One of the great advantages of Perfection City is that we all have time for the cultivation of our higher natures."

"Just now," said Olive, "my husband seems to have no thought in his mind but the cultivation of that field over there. He is at work early and late. No person could possibly work harder for himself or his individual advantage than he does for the Community."

"There's just a case in point," remarked Mary Winkle complacently. "I always thought your husband very narrow in his views. He slaves away at this corn-planting as if that were the chief end and object of his existence. It is all very well to work at times, but working in order to store up food for the body is the lowest possible form that human activity can take."

"It is the most indispensable form," remarked Olive.

"By no means," replied Mary Winkle with precision. "That observation would seem to indicate that you are more narrow even than your husband. The body is merely the servant of the mind: the mind needs to be fed, and it is the food for the mind which your husband appears so careless about providing. Fortunately for Perfection City, Wright has taken thought on that subject. Wright has a very high standard of what is necessary for the mind."

"It appears to me," said Olive with a snap of her black eyes and an ominous red spot on her cheeks, "that if we all lived up to your standard, it might very well happen that by next winter our minds might be uncomfortably full and our stomachs correspondingly empty. If Ezra did not plough and get his land ready for planting as fast as mortal man can, how is the land to be got ready? It doesn't plough itself, does it, even at Perfection City?"

"I see you will have to get rid of many prejudices," observed Mary Winkle. "Of course community-life only comes easy to people who are adapted to it. Wright and I are adapted. We like it. We shall stay here. We shall succeed therefore. You and Brother Ezra will have to go through a season of training first. You both need it. I dare say you may hear something that you will find useful to you to-morrow from Wright. I will just mention to him where your particular blindness seems to lie. Wright is a very profound thinker. He has given great thought to the subject of the Ultimate Perfection of People. He can explain every step in the training of a perfect communist, and show clearly just where everybody has hitherto gone wrong in their attempts to realize their ideal, and exactly what mistakes they have made. I am glad you have come in time to hear his paper; it will be of lasting good to you. You will be able to profit by it, because you are in great need of proper training. I dare say you need it more even than Ezra. For, after all, he must have learned something from us in the year he has been with us."

# CHAPTER IV.

### MADAME MOROZOFF-SMITH.

The Academy at Perfection City was not a pretentious building in anything but in name. It was a plain wooden house, almost square, having a window on three sides and a door on the fourth, facing south. Inside there were several rough benches, two tables, an iron stove, and a large easy chair, with a small desk beside it, upon which stood a pair of candles. There were no curtains and no carpets, absolutely no attempts at beautifying the place. But the board-floor was clean.

Olive dressed herself in a flutter of expectation for her first visit to this abode of wisdom.

"I expect everybody will be there, because they'll all want to see you, little woman," said her husband, who, tired as he was after his day's work, changed his earth-stained clothes for a fresh suit. Olive wore a white dress with lavender ribbons, and looked as fresh as a daisy as she tripped along daintily holding up her skirts. She wore the nattiest of boots over the neatest of feet, altogether a bright and unexpected sight upon the glum-looking prairie. It was a quarter of a mile to the Academy, down a road hardly more than a cart-track, and across a dry gully where there were no stepping stones.

As Ezra had predicted, everybody had turned out to welcome the new bride. Uncle David met her at the door.

"Wal, little girl," he said, "we're all a-looking out for you. Here's Sister Mary Winkle, you've seen her, and this is her husband, Brother Wright."

Olive shook hands with a dark, broad-shouldered man who spoke in snaps as if he had been a dog. He had glittering white teeth.

"We've been looking to have your husband back," he said.

"I'm sure you're very kind," murmured Olive conventionally.

"We needed him for the ploughing," snapped Wright.

"Oh indeed!" said Olive less cordially.

"This is the busy time of the year."

"All times a-year is the busy time in my 'pinion and 'sperience," said Uncle David smiling comprehensively, "but most everyone spares time one way or 'nother to get married if they have a mind that way. Come along an' see Brother and Sister Dummy. That ain't their name, but we call 'em so, they're deaf and mostly dumb now. They're real good folks too."

A sad-eyed red-haired man shook hands with her, and a sad-eyed woman kissed her. They put into her hand a slip of paper on which was written a message of welcome.

"They can talk a little, but they can't hear one mite, and they don't like to talk, because they can't tell when they are whispering and when they are yelling, and it makes strangers jump to hear them sometimes."

Olive felt drawn towards this poor silent pair, but did not know how to express her sympathy. There were others in the room, but before she had time to speak to them the door opened and Madame Morozoff-Smith entered, and from that moment she seemed to see no one else. Madame was a remarkable looking woman. She was tall, large and fair, with keen grey eyes, full red lips, and a mass of pale gold hair rising over a forehead that was broad and smooth. A woman of indeterminate age with an air of youthfulness and command about her. She was dressed in a dark dress and wore a bright bunch of ribbons in her hair. It looked at first sight like a rose, only roses don't grow on the prairie in the month of May. She came straight to where Olive was standing. She gave one the impression of floating, for although a large woman, she walked so lightly as to make no noticeable sound on the wooden floor. Taking Olive's two hands in her warm large grasp, she kissed her on the forehead murmuring "Welcome," and then stepping back she said in a clear voice that vibrated through the room:

"Ah! now I understand that hurried courtship and swift marriage. I see what it was in Brother Ezra's case. It was love at first sight. You are very pretty. I suppose, however, you know that very well. It is a secret seldom kept from young girls."

Olive was so startled by this unexpected address that she blushed to the roots of her black hair. Ezra stood looking down at his little wife smiling with pleasure. He was delighted to think that Madame found her so pretty. He had indeed thought her beautiful from the first moment when his eyes had rested on her, but then he loved her, and it was but natural that in his eyes she should be lovely. Madame, however, judged her unprejudiced, and yet if his delighted heart had room for one regret, it was that Madame's praise had been so very public. If she had only whispered it softly to him in that wonderful voice of hers, which had often caught up his inmost thoughts and clothed them in words of eloquence, how much more precious would the tribute have been. He dismissed the half-formed regret as unworthy, and took himself to task for not exulting at this moment. The meeting of Madame and Olive was an event in his life. Olive, his sweet little rose-bud of a wife, on the one hand, and Madame, his venerated, nay his worshipped, friend, on the other. The one, the companion of his heart: the other, the guide of his mind who embodied in herself all that he held highest in the possibilities of womanhood, his true and noble-hearted friend, his inspired leader. How blest was the portion of him who stood that night the husband of the one, the disciple of the other! Ezra's dark eyes shone with joy, and his square chin quivered with the smiles that lurked about his lips. He was not a handsome man, perhaps, but there was something grand in the large full forehead, strong eyebrows, and deep dark eyes. His massive frame bespoke strength, which in itself has always a great attraction for women.

When Madame had addressed those words to the new sister all the members of the Community had scanned her narrowly, for the opinion of their leader had immense weight with the Pioneers. The men looked at Olive with increased admiration, and the women with envy. Only Uncle David appeared disappointed and wiped his face many times with his red pocket-handkerchief saying, "Wal, wal, now," in a tone of earnest reproof.

After this bewildering introduction in which her vanity had been not a little excited, Olive received a salutary check from the words of Brother Wright.

"Before beginning to read my paper," said he, "I should like to say a few words to the new sister who has come among us. We expect soon to be having new members join us so fast that perhaps we shall not be able to specially mark the entrance of each. But in this case there are peculiar reasons for exhortation. Sister Olive has not joined under ordinary circumstances. She did not, like the rest of us, feel a call to the higher life: she only came out of personal affection for one of the members of the Community."

Olive looked with a shy glance towards her husband, who took her hand in his for a moment, while Uncle David, who sat at the end of the room near Madame, said in a loud voice:

" Quite right, quite right, couldn't ha' had a better reason."

" Therefore it becomes our duty to impress upon our new sister the principles which have been active in forming this Community," said Brother Wright, without paying any heed to Uncle David's interruption. " Perfection City has been founded to teach the world how to live. The old civilization has been tried and found wanting. It is time for a new one. Perfection City is the beginning of a new era. We are the Pioneers of a new world. We shall show the old and worn-out world how to banish evil from life. We cannot perhaps banish all physical evil, and for a time at least there may be sickness even among us, but we shall at once set about freeing ourselves from all the other troubles of life. There is nobody in Perfection City who will get rich, and nobody will ever be poor. We are all alike, and we shall none of us envy our neighbours his belongings, simply because everything belongs to all. The lesson we have to teach is the grandest the world ever saw, and when men know what it is, I foresee a future before Perfection City greater than that of any other city of the world. Rome lasted a good long while, but Rome didn't possess the vital spark of life: Rome wasn't communistic, therefore Rome fell. Perfection City won't fall like that, but will go on teaching the world after we, its founders, are all dead. But our memories will live for the great things that we taught and through our example have made possible."

Brother Wright stopped for a few seconds, and Uncle David said admiringly,

"You have a fine command of words, Brother Wright, and you have a way of making things sound uncommon grand. It always does me good to hear you talk of the grand future of our City; but we'll have to get up some houses, and bigger ones, 'fore folks 'ull believe us."

Uncle David was as simple as a child, or some of his hearers might have suspected a sarcasm in his words.

"Rome wasn't built in a day, as I've heard say," remarked Brother Green, with a strong English accent, "and I shall be glad if our little village ever grows to half its power and honour."

"Brother Green, I should refuse to have anything to say to the founding of another city like Rome," interrupted Brother Wright with decisiveness.

"It seems to me," said Ezra in a shy hesitating

manner, "that what we are here for is to demonstrate, if we can, how a better life can be lived here than is possible in the older communities, where circumstances are too strong and too hampering for people to rise above them. The older civilization has done much, it has raised our race to a high standard. What we want to do is to carry on that work, and above all to bring everyone within reach of the best that life has to offer. The older civilization has left so many stranded ones, who have lost their strength in the wild struggle; while we hope to bring all along equally and give to each a share of happiness. As usual, my friends, when I try to express my ideas I find that someone else has already put them into incomparably finer language than I can ever command. It has been so again. I find that our great poet, Walt Whitman, has said better than I can what I feel. May I quote him to you?

'Have the elder races halted?
Do they droop and end their lesson, wearied over there beyond the seas?
We take up the task eternal, and the burden and the lesson, Pioneers! O pioneers!'"

Ezra sat down after reciting his verse, and his wife looked at him with glowing eyes. He had not said much, but his words had seemed to her so much fuller of thought and feeling than the easy monotonous flow from Brother Wright. That individual himself had not received Ezra's remarks with quite so much delight. It was Brother Wright's nature to see fight and contradiction in all things, even the most pacific. His eyes would flash and his black beard bristle in argument, almost as if he were a dog preparing to fight, and if one might be permitted to liken any Pioneer to one of the canine species, the bull-dog would undoubtedly be the variety most nearly resembling Brother Wright.

"I don't see that we need be beholden to anyone, poet or otherwise," he said sharply, "for our opinions or sentiments. We have found them for ourselves, just as we have founded our City. It is our work, both opinions and practice."

"I think," said Madame, rising and speaking with a deep clear voice, which a slight foreign accent seemed to render only the more attractive, "I think I see better than they do themselves where our two brothers agree. Brother Ezra, with that diffidence which strong natures often exhibit, thought he found in the lines of another man his own ideas more succinctly embodied than they would have been in his own words. Brother Ezra should not doubt his powers. Speech comes slowly to those who most deeply think, but he should consider how much we benefit by his words and how grateful we are to him for them. Brother Wright, it seems to me that you, perhaps, do not sufficiently appreciate the efforts of others who have gone before us on this road. We are not the first who have been discontented with the actual order of things, nor are we the first who have striven to make life brighter and easier. In all ages there have been those penetrated with these thoughts, and in different ways men, and women too, have striven earnestly, devotedly, to realize these ideas. Some indeed have imagined they had found a solution of all doubts and difficulties, and have in perfect good faith and self-satisfaction buried themselves in convents and monasteries and have 'roll'd the psalm to wintry skies,' and have 'built them fanes of fruitless prayer.' We have come to different conclusions by following a different road. We do not shut ourselves out of the world, rather we endeavour to raise it by showing a living example of what may be done now, in this age, by human beings such as we are. But if we are to succeed we must not reject the experience, nor fail to profit by the example, of others who have gone before us and felt earnestly on this subject."

Madame paused for a moment, and her keen glance rested upon the small assembly. Each individual seemed to feel that she was looking at him or at her. Certainly each member was looking intently at her. She seldom made speeches to them; she only interposed her observations, as on this occasion, between the speakers; but the last word usually remained with her.

"Brother Wright, will you now read us your paper, as the evening is passing and we are all anxious to hear it. What is the title and subject?"

"The Ultimate Perfection of Being is the title," said Brother Wright, "and I think that pretty well sums up the subject also."

So apparently thought the audience, which resigned itself to a severe mental excursion into the unknown regions of Brother Wright's imaginative metaphysics. Some of them fell out very soon, finding the road harder to follow than they had foreseen; but Brother Wright kept sturdily on, unheeding the signs of weakness and disaffection as betrayed by movings of feet and stifled yawns.

Olive, not being able to understand what Brother Wright was saying, employed herself in watching Madame, who sat motionless beside her table, resting her head upon her supple white hand. At her feet lay what seemed to be a large brown rug, but was in fact her dog Balthasar, a blood-hound, who always stayed with her and was as gentle as a lamb, notwithstanding his name and breed.

"Brother Green! That's the second time you've snored," suddenly exclaimed Brother Wright in the midst of his reading. Everybody was wide awake in an instant. Madame hid a smile with her hand, but not before Olive had noticed it.

"Brother Green is perhaps tired. His work is very hard," said Madame.

"Well, the fact is I had to put a new point to the ploughshare this morning before I went to fetch my load of iron, and I began work before daybreak. I am very tired."

Brother Green was the blacksmith of Perfection City, an industrious hard-working man who thought life would show him a fairer side on the prairie than it had ever done in the far-away village in Sussex where he was born.

"I think that it might be better to have our gatherings rather shorter now," said Madame softly. "The workers in our little hive are all tired. I wish I could do more of the labour that is needed. I would gladly——"

Madame was interrupted by a sharp rap on the table, a signal from Brother Huntley that he wanted to speak. He was the deaf and dumb man. She instantly rose and bowed to him with singular graciousness. Madame's manner towards the deaf brethren was all that was exquisite. Huntley stood up and began in a voice almost inaudible which rose by sudden degrees to the intensity of a steam-whistle.

"I want to know when we're going to get our corn planted? We're behindhand; most other folk's corn is in already."

"As usual, Brother Huntley has something practical to say," observed Madame.

"He didn't know we were discussing quite another subject, else his remark would have been rude and irrelevant," said Wright, vexed at this cutting into his paper on the ultimate perfection of his and everybody's being.

"I think it would be very useful to see what we can do about the corn," said the blacksmith. "If we are late the chances are there'll be another drought in July, and our crop won't be first-class."

"Is anyone's land ready for planting?" inquired Madame.

"None as I know of, except Brother Dummy's," said Uncle David. "He's more forward nor anybody: always first in work."

"Of course, poor deaf creature! he can't do anything but dumbly work like a——" began Brother Wright.

"My land is ready for planting," burst in Brother Huntley with a scream.

"Then it shall be planted to-morrow," cried Madame. "I'll go myself."

"You!" exclaimed Olive.

"Certainly, child. Don't you think I can work as well as any other woman?"

She rapidly wrote a few words on a slip of paper and passed it to Brother Huntley, who read it, nodded with satisfaction, and said: "Five o'clock in the morning!" in a voice so low that no one knew he was speaking.

"I suppose he begins work about six?" said Madame.

"No, he don't, he's mighty spry," said old Mrs.

Ruby, who lived near the Huntleys. "I hear him a-movin' off with his plough every morning at five by the clock. He's terrible sot on his work."

"Then I shall be there ready to go to work at five o'clock in the morning, and I shall begin by going to bed now, so as to be able to give a good day's work. Good-night, friends all."

She rose, included them all in a sweeping salute and left the room as lightly as she had entered. Balthasar rose and slowly followed her.

When Madame left the room the meeting broke up. No one felt inclined to linger when she was gone. It was from her they drew their interest in each other, as well as their belief in themselves and in Perfection City. She possessed the secret of influencing people without seeming to do so. The thought that she was going out on the land at five in the morning to plant corn made everyone ten times more eager to work than heretofore.

Wright and his independent spouse, Mary Winkle, were infected by her example as they went home.

"Now, Wright, don't you go and do any more essaying till the crop is in. I think people oughtn't to write except in winter time," said Mary Winkle with firmness.

"I never believed in nothing but manual work. Why, if I did, I should be still slaving away on that farm out in Illinois, instead of joining a community here where one can follow the bent of his higher nature, to the advantage of his neighbours as well as of himself," said Wright.

"Well, let that be," said Mary hastily, recognising her own words and oft-expressed opinions, but not quite knowing what to do with them—a predicament not unexampled among theoretical philosophers, "but see and be out on the land to-morrow as early as anyone. Are you ready for the planting? Because I'll go out and plant if you are."

"No, my drills won't be ready for the planting till day after to-morrow."

"Then I'll go and plant on Brother Dummy's piece along with Madame."

"You'd better not. You're not fit for such work. You'll get sick and not be able to cook me any supper when I come home."

"No, I shan't get sick. I ain't going to let any person beat me at work, when I set my mind to it, and she in her long skirts too! I'll show her the advantage of the reformed dress anyhow."

Thus the Wright and Winkle pair on their way home.

"And will she really plant corn?" asked Olive in some curiosity.

"Certainly she will. Madame never despised work."

"Oh! I don't despise work, but she seems such

a fine lady to go out on the land and plant corn just like a negro woman."

"That is one of the things our life here is intended to show, dearie, that no one is too grand for any honest work that he or she is physically capable of performing."

## CHAPTER V.

### CORN PLANTING.

Punctual to the minute, there was Madame with her bag of corn on her left arm, following Brother Huntley and his plough-horses to the field, in the damp white fog of sunrise. Balthasar in deep disgust was there too, as in duty bound, but he had not a wag for anybody. How could a rational dog be in good spirits at that hour of the morning! Madame was dressed in a short calico frock well up to her ankles. Her fair hair was loosely wisped at the back of her head, and a large straw hat, tied down with a green gauze veil, made her look at once comfortable in the fog and ready for the expected sunshine. There were no corn-planters at Perfection City: farm-machinery was not then so plentiful on the prairie as now, and money was if possible scarcer. Corn planting was, therefore, done by hand. Brother Dummy's drills of longitude were already ploughed, and he began on the drills of latitude forthwith. Into the hollows made by the intersection of these two sets of drills Madame was to drop three grains of corn, neither more nor less. It is dizzying work. After walking up and down the drills for hours one becomes oppressed by the never-ceasing square constantly recurring every two steps. The check pattern bewilders you, and you begin to wonder how a chess-man would feel if, endowed with sensibility and the power of motion, he had to march up and down his chess-board, always keeping to the lines for hours at a stretch.

About seven o'clock Mary Winkle came upon the scene and plodded and planted for four hours. The sun was blazing down upon them pitilessly, and the parching south wind blew the fine black dust up from the rich dry soil, until their eyes and ears and noses were full of it.

The field which they were planting was on the extreme verge of the community-land, far away from the houses. These were somewhat clustered towards the centre of the holding, which consisted of two sections or a little over twelve hundred acres. The workers, therefore, were a long way from home, considerably over a mile, and since corn planting entails ceaseless walking through heavy ploughed land, it had been settled that their dinner should be brought out to them, so as to enable the workers to rest during the whole dinner hour. Olive and Mrs. Ruby were to supply the necessary food, and the former, aided by Napoleon Pompey, was to bring it to the field at eleven o'clock. The little grove of locust trees just beginning to grow beside the far spring was the trysting place. Water would thus be handy, and the horses' feed was already put there by the provident Brother Huntley. A little before the hour Olive and her black attendant arrived at the grove, bringing their load of food, and Olive set down her big tin can with a sigh of relief. Her arms ached with carrying it, for it was heavy and the way was long. Napoleon Pompey had carried two cans, each heavier than hers, but the lad seemed to feel no inconvenience from the load. Olive looked at him with envy and thought with contempt of her own muscles which appeared so inefficient. As she unpacked the food, it seemed to her that nothing she had learnt at Smyrna and could best do, was wanted on the prairie, and she remembered with some amusement and not a little bitterness Mary Winkle's words about food for the mind. At this moment she reflected that all the learning in the world was not so much needed by that philosophical lady as the very gross and material food which was being taken out of the heavy tin cans and laid on the grass. The working-party, men, women and horses, arrived while Olive was thus engaged. Mary Winkle instantly sat down and leaned against a tree and threw off her sun-bonnet. Her thin black hair was matted down to her temples, her cheeks were yellow, and her eyes looked dull. Madame also took off her hat and veil and shook up the coil of hair on her head with a sigh of relief.

"Does your head ache too?" said Mary Winkle wearily.

"Not in the least," replied Madame. "A sun-bonnet is a bad shelter against heat. You should wear a good hat, it is far better."

"I wonder how you can bear all that hair on your head. Why don't you cut it off?"

"Why, it is an admirable protection against both heat and cold," said Madame laughing. "It is my greatest comfort." She might have added her greatest beauty.

The food which Olive brought was most appetising, roast chicken, hot corn-bread, and pumpkin pies, with plenty of milk and water to drink. Before eating Madame went to the spring to wash her hands and face, and Mary Winkle sat limply against the tree trunk with her eyes shut.

"Eat something, it will revive you," said Olive, looking with pity upon her sallow cheeks.

"I don't feel hardly able to eat," she said in a weak voice. "It seems to me I don't ever want to open my eyes again."

"You are overworking yourself," said Olive, "you should not attempt this field work: it is beyond your strength."

"What! and let her see me give in?" said Mary Winkle with reviving spirit.

Madame came up at this moment looking as fresh as a lily: she glanced sharply at Sister Mary. "You appear very much exhausted," she remarked.

Sister Mary raised her head and opened her eyes, but did not speak.

"It's a pity you don't take wine," she continued, sitting down and beginning on her piece of chicken with relish. "A good glass of Burgundy would set you up in no time."

Sister Mary herself sat up at this.

"I wouldn't touch wine, no, not if I was dying," she said resolutely.

Madame smiled. "I didn't recommend it because you were dying: wine as everything else is then useless: but because you look weak. I suggested a medicine."

"As a medicine it is worse than useless, and as a drink I scorn to take a rank poison."

"Poisons are sometimes given as medicine, witness strychnine in small doses for certain forms of dyspepsia, and I believe satisfactorily," said Madame.

"Wine is worse than strychnine, because more insidious in its action and more liable to abuse," said Mary Winkle decisively, as she took the tin cup of milk and water handed her by Olive, and drank it with eagerness.

"Well, at all events admit that wine has been of benefit to you on this occasion," observed Madame smiling. "I merely mentioned it to you, and you look already revived and more like yourself. Doesn't she, Sister Olive?"

"It was the milk and water did it," said Sister

Mary Winkle hurriedly, at which Madame smiled again.

Brother Dummy and Napoleon Pompey now came up to the group of women. They had been watering and unharnessing the horses who were at the present moment munching their corn. The white man, although dirty as a ploughman would be after half a day's hard work, sat down promptly beside Mary Winkle and helped himself to a leg of chicken: the negro boy stood aside doubtfully, eyeing the group and the food with longing looks.

"Come along, N. P.," said Olive brightly, "sit down there." She pointed to a place on the other side of Mary Winkle, where there seemed a good opening in front of a huge piece of corn-bread.

"No, if you please," said Sister Mary, rising to her feet with resentment.

"Why, what's the matter?" asked Olive flushing with surprise. "Napoleon Pompey won't bite you."

"I have never sat down to eat beside a negro, and I don't feel inclined to begin now."

"Let the lad sit beside me," said Madame gently. "I have seen people of too many shades of colour and no colour to mind a little extra dash of black. Come here, boy, come and have this piece of bread and meat."

Napoleon Pompey grinning with all his white teeth sprang to the place beside Madame, and buried those same teeth eagerly in his chunk of bread. Mary Winkle sat down again and leaned against the tree. Olive's face took a deeper tinge of red and her eyes snapped.

"Do you consider yourself made of such fine clay that it won't bear contact with a negro?" she asked hotly. "It seems to me a little of what used to be called Christian charity might come in useful here. I never aspired to the heights of Perfection City people, but I never refused the rights of brotherhood to the negro simply because of the curl of his hair or the colour of his skin."

"I am quite willing to give them all their rights and will be glad to see them educated and all that, but I never sat at dinner with a negro, and I am not going to begin now," said Mary Winkle setting her thin pale lips with the utmost stubbornness.

"Well, I call it perfectly monstrous," retorted Olive, "and you setting yourself up to show the better life and all the rest of it! I should have thought the first thing to do before teaching the highest perfection was to practise the simplest justice."

"And you, Sister Olive," said Madame's cool sweet voice, "will have to learn to respect the prejudices of other people even when they run counter to your most cherished theories. I do not myself share the feeling of repulsion that Sister Mary has in this case, but I respect it. I would suggest to you to do the same. It is an inconvenient fact, perhaps, that people do not all think alike, but it is one that must be resolutely faced nevertheless."

Olive was silent under this reproof, but she looked angrily at Mary Winkle from time to time, and revenged herself by feeding up Napoleon Pompey and petting him to an alarming extent, much to the delight of that young darkie who ate until he seemed to ooze out unctuous joy.

Brother Dummy ate, as he worked, silently, conscientiously, continuously. Olive was amazed at the amount he seemed able to consume, while of milk and water he drank half a gallon or thereabouts.

"How can he do it?" said Olive in astonishment.

"You forget," replied Madame, "that he has been following that plough for six long hours, and the dry wind raised such a dust around him that he must have swallowed a vast quantity of it in the course of the day. It takes a good deal to slake the thirst after such a dust visitation as that."

When Brother Dummy had eaten and drunk his fill he lay down on the grass and went instantly to sleep. The three women looked at him for a moment or two.

"He seems to have very little enjoyment in his life," said Olive compassionately.

"But then he has also few sorrows," said Madame. "The high lights are wanting, perhaps, but so are the dark shadows. His life is like a grey landscape. It has a beauty of its own, but not everyone can see it."

"To live in eternal silence seems to me the most awful curse," said Olive.

"I can imagine many a worse one," replied Madame, looking out from among the few bare trees away across the open prairie.

"What could be worse?"

"Well, for example, to know that someone you loved did not love you. To have to shut up your heart within iron doors, and never open them to let it out. That would be worse than to be denied the power of speech, which after all can now be supplemented in many ways by artificial means. Brother Huntley is not actively unhappy, I should judge. He and his wife have always appeared to me to be a very united couple."

"They cannot quarrel, at all events," said Olive.

"No, not, at least, in the ordinary way," replied Madame.

When Brother Dummy awoke after his little snooze, he got up, looked at the sun to see what time of day it was, and then signed to Napoleon Pompey to rouse up. That young person was lethargic, owing to his anaconda-like meal, accordingly Brother Dummy roused him with his foot. The darkie rolled over and said "Yah!" and started for the horses, who were nodding over their corncobs, now nibbled down to the smallest dimensions. Olive, whose resentment at the slight put upon Napoleon Pompey by Mary Winkle urged her to identify herself with the negro boy, walked away with him and Brother Dummy to watch the hitching up. Madame employed herself in throwing scraps of bread to Balthasar, who would have much preferred eating the chicken bones, only that was a debauch not permitted to a dog of his manners. Mary Winkle looked hopelessly along those weary furrows, up and down which it would be her duty to march again, dropping her seeds of corn as before.

"Are you going to work all the afternoon?" she asked of her companion.

"Yes, I think so. We shall get this field planted and covered in by sun-down, I should think. And that will be a great piece of work done. We cannot afford to let the individualists beat us at corn planting, can we? We must do at least as well as they, and I should hope we might do better."

"I don't know how you can stand so much heat and hard work," said Mary, "and in that dress too. Why, if I were to attempt to work in long skirts I should be dead in a week."

"I don't mind my dress at all," said Madame. "It never bothers me. I don't think about it."

"But don't you think about it when your back aches?"

"It never does."

"I don't understand it," says Mary once more.

"I suspect that the reason you American women find your dress such a burden is because you are so weak yourselves," said Madame.

"American women accomplish as much or more than any others, I should say," observed Mary.

"Precisely, but not from their muscular strength. They work out of their nerves, and that is why they never last any length of time."

Madame finished her day's work at six o'clock, and then walked home humming a German dance tune to herself. Mary Winkle stopped at four o'clock, and dragged herself home to bed with a fearsome headache, still puzzling how it was that her perfect dress had not done better for her in that day's trial. She did not know that all her scientific dressing was as nothing compared with the robust vitality, which Madame brought with her from another land, and which, running in such vigorous beats through her blood, was inherited from generations of strong healthy ancestors. Madame's father was a Russian colonel noted for his size and strength and also for his wildness. Her mother was a pretty English girl, who had nothing to bequeath to her daughter but health, personal beauty, and this piece of advice: "Never stake your happiness on any man, it always brings disaster to the woman." Mary Winkle's mother, on the other hand, was a nervous invalid at thirty, and her father was a dyspeptic dietetic reformer, who pinned his salvation on never eating salt. Small wonder, therefore, that the daughter of the one pair should be able to plant corn all day long and walk lightly home at evening, while the offspring of the other pair could do only three quarters of a day's work, after which headache and nervous exhaustion.

## CHAPTER VI.

#### NON-RESISTANCE.

It was the custom of the Pioneers to send once a week to Union Mills in order to do their necessary marketing and to get the post, which came there twice a week from Kansas City by stage-coach. The subject of the post was one that had been rather hotly debated at Perfection City, although to the outsider it would seem a very harmless topic, and not fruitful of division. The fact was, however, that there was only one member of the Community who showed any eagerness about getting letters regularly and often, and that member was Madame. She indeed did receive a most unconscionable number of letters and periodicals, so the other members thought. She got several American Magazines, such as the Atlantic Monthly and Harper's, but she also received English papers, and French ones, and occasionally German ones as well. The Community thought, but did not dare to give public expression to the thought, that Madame should have rested content with the mental sustenance provided by themselves for home consumption.

Brother Wright in particular felt himself equal to the task of providing everybody with all they needed in the way of correct views upon even the highest subjects. But Madame, although she listened with politeness and apparent attention to what he had to say, found this sustenance too meagre for the wants of her nature. Moreover she took a deep interest in the affairs of the outside world, an interest almost offensive to persons who prided themselves upon having risen above the world and all its concerns. It was really humiliating to think that the leading spirit of their Community should occupy her mind with the relations between Prussia and Austria, when such questions as affected the future of humanity and of Perfection City were what filled their souls. She even evinced a keen interest in the career and personality of the Prussian minister, Bismarck, and that, too, when Brother Wright was willing to give her the light of his thoughts upon all really important questions. It was painful to the feeling of the Pioneers, who were all in all to themselves and wished to be so to others, but they had to put up with it, since Madame was their leader and, moreover, the only one who had a purse with some money in it. Ezra was the only member of the Community who sided with Madame in her taste for reading the new books and the latest periodicals. He and she had that taste, with many others, in common, and it drew them together in an especial degree. On his last trip East during the winter, when he had been so unexpectedly delayed, as they now knew, by meeting with his fate in the shape of Olive, one of his commissions had been to bring back a box of books, which were now arranged in neat shelves in Madame's private sitting-room. And yet notwithstanding all these books, a hundred or more, the steady stream of papers, periodicals, and magazines continued as before, and had to be fetched regularly from Union Mills.

The brethren took it in turns to go to the town, which was some ten miles distant, and they always combined some useful business with the fetching of the letters. Brother Wright was a frequent messenger, for he liked going better than Ezra did, while of course Brother Dummy was precluded by his affliction from going, and Brother Carpenter was hopelessly unable to drive horses. Some of the women generally contrived to find an excuse for going to Union Mills, for women like to get away from the petty cares of house and home, a peculiarity from which the sisters of Perfection City were by no means exempt. In particular Mrs. Ruby, invariably called Aunt Ruby, loved to go. She thus got a chance of seeing new faces and talking with new people. She would not for worlds have confessed that she was tired of the restricted society of Perfection City, but she knew so well what each had to say, that it was refreshing to go out sometimes into the world and meet people whose ideas could not always be guessed beforehand.

It so happened that the day after the corn planting it became necessary to go to Union Mills in order to take a grist of corn to be ground. Madame suggested that Brother Wright should go, while Brother Dummy took up his plough-handles and finished the field the former was preparing for the corn. Mary Winkle, still prostrated by the previous day's hard work, urged her spouse to go, "For then," said she, "if you ain't here I needn't get any dinner. I'll just send Willette over to Sister Olive's for dinner, and I needn't stir till milking time." This seemed a happy arrangement, and her husband set off shortly after breakfast, picking up Aunt Ruby as he passed her cottage.

"Be you lonesome living in that house by yourself?" asked Brother Wright as they jogged along over the prairie, for it had struck him as very lonely that morning as he drove up.

"No, no, I ain't lonely, least not most whiles," answered Aunt Ruby, an alert little old woman, not unlike a bird in her quick movements. "In the summer-time there's allus the chickens to see to an' feed an' ten', an' chickens is powerful spry an' talkin' birds. They most allus has somethin' to scold an' chatter 'bout, chickens an' hens has, an' cocks. Then in the winter I hev the clock tickin' loud o' evenin's, an' that's most as good as a pusson in the room, an' there's allus the cat, an' mostly the kettle singin' on the stove. Come to think on't, there's a heap o' company in a house like mine, if you on'y has ears to hear an' un'erstan' what is said by beasts an' things."

Yet notwithstanding this " heap o' company " Aunt Ruby dearly loved a good gossip with the saddler's wife at Union Mills, whenever that luxury was attainable. On the present occasion Aunt Ruby had a real good time, for Brother Wright was delayed longer than usual, first in order to get some harness mended, and afterwards to have a shoe replaced that suddenly showed signs of coming off one of the horses. Thus it was very near sun-down before they left Union Mills. Aunt Ruby, owing in large measure to her gossip, and also partly to an exceptionally strong cup of tea, was in a highly nervous and excitable frame of mind.

Had Brother Wright, she asked, heard of that rumour about the Cherokees? And did he think there was any danger of their leaving their Reservation and going on the war-path? Brother Wright, who had a poor opinion of Indians, and a worse one of the way in which the white men had treated them, thought on the whole that the rumour might be considered false. This comforted Aunt Ruby, to whom the word " Injun " suggested torture and death and all sorts of horrors. She remained comforted until she remembered that other rumour—about the raid of border ruffians from out of Missouri. Brother Wright thought it highly probable that this rumour might prove to be true. Missouri men had raided Kansas more than once, and it was possible they might do so again at any moment. With coversation such as this they came to the end of the daylight and the beginning of the trees around Cotton Wood Creek about the same time.

"I shall be glad when we are safe over this ford and out of the dark wood beyond," said Brother Wright, trying to urge his horses along, but he had a heavy load of timber and coal and some iron bars for smith-work.

"Ain't it near here that those people over beyond Jacksonville got robbed?" asked Aunt Ruby, nervously peering about in the gloom with her weak old eyes. At this moment some distant creature made a shrill scream or howl.

"Oh! what was that," exclaimed Aunt Ruby nervously.

"That was a prairie wolf, I guess," answered Brother Wright quietly.

Silence followed, except for the creaking of the waggon, the straining of the horses at their traces, and an occasional clang made by one of the bars of iron which was not sufficiently wedged up with hay.

"If those Missouri border ruffians came to Perfection City, do you reckon our principles would save us from being robbed?" asked Aunt Ruby. "Most everybody knows as we are non-resistants."

"I don't think our principles would stand in the way of a Missouri man. More likely they would take advantage of them. They are mean cusses, and are used to riding rough-shod over principles and rights. It is a recognised thing everywhere that women and children are non-resistants, yet that does not save 'em from being raided and robbed by border ruffians."

"And you think they would rob us, peaceful folks as ha'n't no arms nor nothin'?" asked Aunt Ruby anxiously.

"I guess they would try," replied Brother Wright.

"Then I think as we oughter reconsider our principles a mite," said Aunt Ruby. "For if we are robbed and killed by folks as can't un'erstan' the higher life, we shan't be able to teach the world nothin'. An' what's the good o' principles when you're dead an' gone an' undergroun'?"

"That is so," assented Brother Wright.

"I didn't never think on't in this light afore," said Aunt Ruby. "It 'pears to me as how we should meet together an' try an' settle some way as how we can keep our principles an' yet live on the prairie."

"I guess you've pretty nearly said the truth," said Brother Wright.

"What we hev to do is to live here an' show 'em our principles at work, an' not die straightway afore we've done anything to improve mankind. That's my view," said Aunt Ruby. "What do you think, Brother Wright?"

Instead of answering Brother Wright pulled up short and looked intently in front of him.

"What's the matter?" exclaimed Aunt Ruby in a high-pitched voice of alarm.

"Hush!" replied her companion, "don't make a noise."

Aunt Ruby's heart began to beat violently. "Do you see anything?" she asked in a whisper.

"I see a man over there by the road, sitting on horseback with his right arm out pointing towards the waggon."

"Oh! brother, I wish you had a carnal weapon of defence," said Aunt Ruby in a shaking voice.

"I have," replied Brother Wright, pulling an uncommonly useful-looking Colt's revolver from his breeches pocket. "I always carry one in case of Injuns."

Again they sat silent for a moment, the horses shook their heads, and one of them stamped a foot.

"Who goes there?" hailed Brother Wright in a loud defiant voice. "Drop that right arm of yours or I'll fire."

No answer.

The figure sat motionless, the right hand still raised in that menacing attitude.

"I am a man of my word," said Brother Wright, rising to his feet and sighting his revolver steadily on the figure, while to Aunt Ruby he said, "Hold on tight, the horses will jump."

A shot rang out on the still night air. The horses nearly jumped out of their skins with fright, and would certainly have run away, only the waggon was very heavy, and they decided to run in different directions. Hence they only jerked each other almost to the ground and then stood still amazed and trembling.

"Better make sure," said Brother Wright, emptying another barrel at the figure which appeared to remain motionless in the uncertain foggy light. This time the horses came to the same conclusion and tried to turn round abruptly, but the attempt was expertly frustrated by Brother Wright and a cowhide whip of exceptional stinging power. Having thus reduced the horses to reason, he again turned his attention to the figure and saw with amazement that it still sat on horseback in the same spot.

"Well, I swan!" said Brother Wright, rubbing his eyes. "That beats all! It can't be a mortal man, or he would have either dropped or returned fire. I guess I'll drive on and do no more shooting this time."

He stowed his pistol away in his pocket and drove on.

"Hadn't you better keep the weapon handy?" suggested Aunt Ruby. "You might lay it down in my lap, if you like."

"No, thank'ee," replied Brother Wright. "I don't generally give that sort of thing to women to hold for me."

He pulled up at a little opening just near the

ford, where the faint light of a crescent moon showed between the bare branches of the trees, and a sort of water-fog hung along the elder bushes by the banks.

"This is the spot he was standing," remarked Wright, "the exact spot. I guess I'll just look and see if there is any trail. The ground is soft about here and should show up pretty clear."

He descended from the waggon and carefully examined the side of the road, but could see nothing. There was a large stump with a broken branch sticking out which attracted his attention, and he walked around it a couple of times, surveying it critically in the uncertain light.

"Well, I swan!" he exclaimed, after the third inspection. "I didn't think I could have been mistaken."

Then he climbed back into the waggon, and said, "Gee-up!"

"Did you fin' any tracks o' robbers?" asked his companion anxiously.

"No," replied Brother Wright, "no tracks of robbers, but I lighted on the trail of a doggauned fool. Guess we'll not say much about the attack made on our waggon, at Little Cotton Wood Creek."

"I won't mention it at all," remarked Aunt Ruby, "'cause it might frighten the folks up to Perfection City an' make 'em uneasy 'bout coming to Union Mills."

Brother Wright only chuckled in reply, possibly

because his whole attention was required at this juncture to get his horses and waggon safely through the water, for it was certainly very dark in that bottomland. Once the creek was crossed and the high prairie reached, it became easy enough to see by the light of the new moon and the stars, and the pair reached Perfection City in safety, although very late.

Brother Wright was very eager to unravel the mystery of that horseman at the ford on Little Cotton Wood Creek, so he made a private expedition thither on horseback as soon as he could frame an excuse for a morning's absence. He went to the place whence he had first seen the alarming stranger, half closed his sharp grey eyes, and looked.

"Well, I swan!" he remarked, as this expression seemed somehow to relieve his feelings. By daylight there was nothing suspicious to be seen, but the old stump with the broken branch sticking out from it straight towards the spectator. Brother Wright surveyed this stump critically and came to the conclusion that with the help of darkness, a slight mist, a new moon, and a nervous companion, the old stump might take on an alarming aspect. He rode up to the stump, got off his horse, and examined it.

"I should like to know that I hit him plumb with both bullets anyhow," remarked he, with a grin most unbecoming to a Perfection City non-resistant. He had hit "him" plumb, but so had other people, and the amazed Brother Wright counted no less than seventeen bullet holes, both old and new, in the body of that long suffering stump.

"Well, I be jiggered!" said Brother Wright as he mounted his horse. "What a sight of blamed fools there must be in the world!" and with this comforting reflection he rode home, and ever after held his peace about the episode on the ford of Little Cotton Wood Creek. And so likewise did Aunt Ruby, that talkative old lady. But sometimes, when she and Brother Wright looked into each other's eyes, they grinned a little sheepishly, showing that the recollection of it had not quite faded from their minds.

## CHAPTER VII.

#### WILLETTE.

WILLETTE, the only child of the Wright and Winkle pair, was a young person of considerable character, which had undergone little of the attempted modification which we call education. At the time of Olive's arrival at Perfection City this child was about eleven years old, and was as wild a specimen of a girl as could be easily found even on the prairie. Her mother had endeavoured to clothe her in garments known as the "reform-dress," and had made her a suit of lilac calico, consisting of short tunic, and full-gathered trousers of the prescribed pattern. Willette had put on these things and had promptly complained of "scratchiness" around the neck and arm-holes, owing probably to deficiency of skill on the part of her mother in the making of the said garments. Shortly afterwards, being called upon to do some cattle-hunting, Willette had set out in all the pride of her new clothes to ride down some young steers who were proving refractory. The steers took shelter in the bottom-land along Little Cotton Wood Creek, and skilfully hid themselves in the brushwood there, among the trailing wild vines and the spiky wilder plums which formed a very good barrier against pursuing man. Willette plunged bravely into the brush, and after a fierce struggle returned with one steer and half her dress. The other half remained in the brush along with the rest of the steers. Repeated onslaughts reduced her almost to nakedness, but she brought home the full complement of steers and an abundant assortment of scratches on her legs. After that Willette had enough of her mother's system of dress, and accordingly she evolved one of her own.

"I ain't a-goin' to cattle-hunt in no more o' your cobwebs, Ma," explained this young person. "I reckon I'll go a-ridin' like a boy next time."

Willette appropriated one of her father's pants made of the material known as hickory, which is supposed to resist any tear or strain. The current legend attached to real out-and-out hickory is as follows. A farmer arrayed in hickory was one day rooting out old stumps from a newly-cleared field with a new patent plough. He came to a regular stunner which jerked the plough clean out of the land. He backed up, took a good hold of the plough-handles, gave a mighty yell to the horses, and drove the plough clean through the stump, which split open in the middle. The plough and the man passed through, but the stump closed up again and caught his hickory trousers. The horses strained at the collar, but the man would not let go of the plough, nor would the stump relinquish its grasp of the hickory trousers. So he rested his horses a spell, took a big breath, and said "Hallelujah!" whereupon the horses went forward with a bound and brought plough, man, trousers, and stump along with them!

It was a garment of this incomparable material that Willette appropriated to her use. She cut off the legs until the length suited her stature, regardless of the fit of the waist, clothed the upper part of her body in a pink check shirt, put a boy's cap upon her head, and announced her intention of henceforth dressing like that. She was a chip of the old block with a vengeance, and Mary Winkle, after one affrighted gasp, was obliged to admit that her own principles, as put into practice by her daughter, were too much for her. Wright laughed immensely, and said she was a boy now and would do firstrate.

Willette was totally uneducated, could not write her name and could scarcely read, but she did not lack for intelligence. She knew the hour of the day, by looking at the sun, as well as a negro, and she could distinguish a horse from a cow at four miles distance. She knew every beast for miles around, and to whom it belonged, and could remember for a month every cow she had come across on the prairie and which way it was heading. She understood the moods and intentions of all kinds of animals almost as if she was one of the species herself, and she never was at fault on a cattle-trail.

Olive found immense amusement in talking to Willette, who expressed herself with the utmost freedom upon all subjects in language which would have done credit to a nigger. The child, on the other hand, had a supreme contempt for Olive's abilities and attainments, which seemed ludicrously deficient, but felt a kindly patronising sort of regard for her, and liked to look at her pretty face and touch her smooth round cheeks. The pair were therefore often together, and Willette undertook to teach her friend to ride, provided she would get some sensible clothes and ride in the only way that Willette imagined it possible for a two-legged human being to bestride a quadruped. Olive therefore made herself a bewitching riding-habit with Turkish trousers, and rode a high-peaked Mexican saddle, out of which even a sack of meal could not tumble if it tried. As soon as Olive began to feel confidence in herself and her horse, she enjoyed the riding immensely. She claimed the refusal of a horse on every possible opportunity when one could be spared from the farm-work. Ezra, delighted to see her so pleased with a healthy exercise, encouraged her to go cattle-hunting with Willette, and enjoyed the spirited reports which she used to bring home from these exhilarating expeditions.

"I do wish I had a pony of my very own which I could take out whenever I wanted a ride, and which would be always there for me," said Olive one day to Ezra after she had been riding by herself on Rebel. Ezra was hoeing up the newly sprouted sweet-corn, and the horses were not at work on the land. In his inmost heart he re-echoed the wish, and would at that moment have given anything to be an individualist and be able to say: " Darling, I'll buy you a pony with the first load of corn I sell." He looked at his pretty wife's glowing cheeks and sparkling eyes, and thought with a groan that he was tied by his principles and prevented by them and the public opinion of the Community from giving his wife this enjoyment. It was the first time that his heart had come into conflict with the perfect theories of Perfection City, and he was amazed and disturbed to find how very much he was vexed by them. Fortunately Olive dismissed the idea of a pony of her own as an unattainable bliss, and contented herself with chance rides on Rebel and Queen Katherine, the two horses which inhabited Ezra's stable and were generally used by him on his side of the community-land.

Olive's courage and spirit of independence, fostered by a very mild-tempered horse, grew apace. She soon felt able to dispense with the escort and instruction of Willette and go cattle-hunting alone. She learned quickly enough to know the sixty head of cattle belonging to the Community, and where to look for them. The cattle, which consisted of the usual mixture of milch cows, steers, yearlings, and calves, had been bought at different times and were apportioned to the different families in rough division, chiefly because each woman liked to have the cows she was to milk, driven up to her own fence near to her own house to save trouble. The cattle, consequently, seemed to have become intensely individualistic in their tendencies, and absolutely refused to graze in common. Each bell-cow led off her own herd of steers and yearlings where she thought best on the prairie, and it was seldom that any two of those "leading ladies" chose to go to the same spot. If they did they generally quarrelled and fought a bit. Cattle-hunting, therefore, became a sufficiently diversified occupation in which the unexpected frequently occurred.

One day it happened that Olive and Diana, now old enough to run with her on her expeditions, had been to the head of Little Cotton Wood Creek to look for a cow that had hidden away her calf there, after the manner of prairie cows. Olive found the truant and the "little stranger," along with half a dozen young cattle, and was driving them slowly homewards, when she became convinced from Rebel's demonstrations that something was annoying him under the flap of his saddle. In fact he was constantly trying to bite Olive's leg in a way which agitated her not a little. Accordingly she resolved to take off the saddle and make an inspection. She dismounted, undid the girths, and lifted off the heavy Mexican saddle. Rebel, who had always hitherto regarded this proceeding as indicating immediate liberty, no sooner felt the saddle removed than he took a base advantage of Olive, and kicking up his heels bounded away from her. She set the saddle in the grass and walked pacifically after Rebel, held out a deceitful hand and called him endearing names. Rebel listened to her honeyed words with his ears flat on his neck, and as soon as she came near, again kicked up his heels and bounded off.

Diana considering all this a joke in which a puppy might lend valuable assistance, now pranced forward with energetic barks, and the cows and calves deeming themselves to be driven with fierceness, set up a lumbering trot across the prairie, the new-made mother every now and then diving ineffectually after Diana with a plunge and a snort. A stampede had set in among the animals, and Olive sat down and cried with vexation and alarm. Her home showed clear and distinct against the horizon just four miles in a bee-line from where she sat shedding her ineffectual tears. Now Diana, although a feminine creature and also a puppy, and therefore endowed with a double dose of original foolishness, was likewise a dog, and consequently amenable to the highest inspirations of a noble nature. Having therefore in her character of puppy worried and distracted the animals to her heart's content, she suddenly felt bound to exhibit some of the better sides of her nature, among which remains forever pre-eminent fidelity to the master. Seeing that Olive was not in the scrimmage, Diana turned her back resolutely upon the delights of snapping at calves' heels, and putting her nose to the ground raced straight back to Olive weeping in the grass. After an apologetic wriggle Diana sat down and looked at Olive. Now no philosopher or other mortal has ever succeeded in being as wise as a tired puppy can look. Therefore when Olive in spite of her woe caught sight of Diana's face and attitude, she burst into a laugh in the midst of her tears, whereupon the latter sprang merrily up and licked her face. Thus comforted, Olive arose, and then became aware that she didn't know where the saddle was. She had neglected to mark its position in any way when going on that deceitful embassy to Rebel, but indeed it would not have been easy to mark the position of the saddle. The grass was in its greatest summer height, and there was neither bush nor tree anywhere for miles around. There was not even a hillock or knoll of ground to give individuality to one spot more than another, all was the relentless rolling prairie—a vast grassy sea where one billow was exactly like a hundred others.

Olive was in dismay. Here was a fresh cause for tribulation, for the saddle was new and expensive, and moreover it belonged to the Community. She would not have minded facing Ezra with a tale of any sort of disaster or loss, for she knew he would kiss her and pet her and say, "Never mind, darling, don't grieve, it doesn't matter two jack-straws." But a community-saddle was quite another matter, and Olive shrank from the ordeal of community-anger at the loss of its saddle, and community-contempt for her carelessness in unsaddling on the prairie without putting the reins over her arm. She perceived now that anyone but a fool would have taken that simple precaution against disaster. "I'm not fit to live on the prairie," sobbed Olive to herself. "My education is no use to me, and I have not got the wits of that boy-girl Willette. Diana, you idiot, why don't you help me?"

This reproach was addressed to the puppy, who was wallowing blissfully in the grass and thus refreshing herself after her scamper. Olive began to walk aimlessly up and down in the hope of stumbling on the saddle, and Diana began to do likewise, but with far more system. Diana's researches were speedily crowned with success, and she soon sat down to an uninterrupted gnaw at the flap of the big Mexican saddle. Becoming at length aware of the disappearance of Diana, Olive called to her, and the puppy reared a mischievous face over the grass some twenty yards away. Going to the spot, Olive perceived the saddle and also the depredations of Diana's sharp teeth upon the flap. She whipped the dog with a stirrup leather most ineffectually and then said:

"What's to be done now?" but Diana, feeling that her efforts had been badly rewarded, made no suggestions.

Indeed Olive's plight after finding the saddle was

considerably worse than before. The thing was very heavy. Mexican saddles are built on wood, large, strong and ponderous, and weigh heavier and heavier in proportion to the distance one carries them. Olive put it on her shoulders and began to see stars, she then tried her head and found that position still worse. She dragged it along by a stirrup-leather and found she was ruining it. Then she sat down and cried, which was the most useless effort she had made. What was she to do? If she were to leave the saddle and walk home she would never be able to find it again. There was absolutely nothing to mark the spot. By this time the cattle were distant specks moving solemnly homewards, with Rebel decorously following in the rear. Olive decided to remain where she was until Rebel and the cattle, by their arrival without her, should have given the alarm, which would bring Ezra and the rest of the Community to the rescue, somewhere about the middle of the night, she supposed. It would be humiliating, but she thought it would be better than abandoning the saddle which she could not possibly carry. She sat down to wait with what patience she could for rescue and humiliation. There was nothing to expect along that weary stretch of grassy sea, and yet Olive kept looking and looking away to the north, east, south, and west. By and by she beheld a horseman coming up from the distant west and holding a slanting course which would carry him past Perfection City some mile or so to the north.

She resolved to intercept this man and ask his aid, so she stood up and signalled wildly with her hat. Of course he saw her instantly, although he was a couple of miles away, and equally of course he at once turned his horse towards her and set off at a gallop. People on the prairie ask and give help freely, and Olive had not the slightest hesitation in calling this unknown horseman up to her aid, although she had not the remotest idea who he might be. Probably he was a cattle-hunter like herself, at any rate a man and a horse would be able to give her and her saddle effectual assistance. The man galloped steadily on and soon took the ordinary appearance: big hat, red shirt, riding boots, belt with probably a revolver somewhere in it. He slowed up a little as he came near and seemed to be very intently looking at Olive.

"I am very sorry to have troubled you," began Olive.

"Don't mention it. I shall be delighted if I can be of use," said the man, taking off his big hat.

They both stopped short and looked hard at each other, for their speech had mutually revealed the fact that they were a lady and a gentleman, a most uncommon encounter on the Kansas prairie beyond the last bit of cultivated land.

"Have you had an accident? Are you hurt?" asked the man, jumping off his horse and mechanically slinging the bridle-rein over his left arm, as Olive noted with some self-reproach. She told him what had happened, and she saw a smile creep round his mouth and light up his blue eyes.

"That is easily remedied. I feared you must have been thrown," said he. "Just mount my horse. He's quiet. I'll take you home."

"But the saddle," said Olive looking very anxiously at that burden.

"Oh! that's nothing," said the stranger. "I'll carry it on my arm."

"You must not dream of such a thing. I could not think of allowing it. You are very kind, I am sure, but if you would take up the saddle in front of you that is all I want. The saddle is the only difficulty. I can walk quite well. I live in that house over there on the brow of the bluff. It is not far, but I could not carry that terrible saddle."

"Why, that's Perfection City, where the Communists live," said he, looking at her curiously.

"Yes, I live there," replied Olive with a slight blush, noting the look.

"And are you a communist, if I may presume to ask the question?" queried the stranger.

"My husband was one of the founders of the—the —of Perfection City," said Olive, valiantly determined to defend the absent.

"But you are not one of the original members. You are surely a new-comer. I know most of them, by sight at all events."

"I am Mrs. Weston," replied Olive with dignity.

The stranger again took off his hat, as if this were an introduction.

"I have seen your husband then, a magnificent specimen of manhood, to judge from the only example I had of his physical strength."

Olive felt at once mollified. Meanwhile, the stranger had shortened the stirrup-leathers of his horse, and turning to Olive he said,

"And now, Mrs. Weston, allow me to give you a hand up to mount you on my big horse. He is quite gentle and I will hold the bridle."

Olive hesitated. "I don't like to take your horse," she said. "If you would be so kind as to leave the saddle——"

"No, no, you must not deprive me of the pleasure of your company," interposed the stranger. "We will manage the saddle all right. Just spring up. Your riding-habit is admirably adapted for prairie life, and the prettiest I ever saw. Pardon my bluntness, but I am so little used to society, I fear I am very rough."

"You don't fear anything of the sort," replied Olive quickly. "You are perfectly aware that your manners are infinitely superior to the article in general use hereabouts."

The man laughed pleasantly at this sally. "Well, let me amend my pleading," said he, "and say, it is so long since I met a lady in these wilds, and that is true enough, Heaven knows!"

Olive mounted the big horse with the dextrous help of his hand and signed to him to give her the saddle.

"I couldn't think of it," said he, thrusting his arm under the saddle and hoisting it on to his shoulder. "It would be unspeakably uncomfortable for you to hold, with the stirrups whacking you at every step."

"Then you shall put it on the horse's neck in front of me, or I'll hop down this instant. It's bad enough to appropriate your horse without making you carry my saddle as well."

Seeing her so determined, he, with a slight show of reluctance, placed the saddle on the neck of his horse, who after a shake or two submitted to the burden, and so they eventually turned homewards.

"I suppose you are not surprised that we settlers out here take considerable interest in your experiment in communism," remarked the man as they walked along.

"No doubt anything out of the common excites comment," said Olive guardedly, "but I should not have thought you could be classed as a settler out here. I have seen a good many, and know the type."

She felt interested in the man and curious to know who he was, he seemed so utterly different from all those she had hitherto met.

"I have lived here, nevertheless, for some years now. I have a farm on the north side of Big Cotton

Wood Creek. My name is Cotterell. Have you ever heard it?"

"No, I never heard the name, but then I've only been here a very short time, only two months. I—that is, we came in May," said Olive blushing somewhat.

The stranger smiled a winning smile and looked up at her face as he answered,

"I see you have only just come, and come as a bride to Perfection City. It has a very suitable sound in that connection."

He again lifted his hat, and Olive blushed more vividly still.

"The prairie does not seem a very hopeful place for experiments in perfection," continued the stranger. "To my eyes it looks a most God-forsaken place, but under certain circumstances I should be disposed to modify that view."

"I think any place will do to try and live a good life in, and that is what is aimed at in our little Community," said Olive, standing bravely to her defence.

He was silent for a time and then spoke again.

"Any place can be made better by the presence of a good woman, I think."

"We want to show how it is possible to banish some of the evil out of life," said Olive, marshalling the expressions she had heard at the Academy with what skill she could.

"With some it is only necessary to be what God

made them in order to banish evil from their presence," said he.

"And we have a very noble woman as leader," said Olive not quite sure of his meaning.

"Ah, indeed! You praise her, that should count for much. There are very mixed reports about her character on the prairie. Many seem to dislike and distrust her."

"As for that I suppose there are mixed reports about us all," observed Olive impartially.

"Indeed there are. For instance, it is most confusing what people say concerning the extent to which you carry your communistic theories. Some assert that there is no limit and that you are logical."

"I don't understand what you mean," said Olive, knitting her brows.

"I presume now that the land is held in common?"

"Yes, certainly, and the farm implements and the horses and cows," answered Olive.

"All those don't really touch the question. You live in separate houses, I believe."

"Of course we do. I should hate not having my own little house. It would be like a hotel or a penitentiary for all to live under one roof. I wouldn't do it for worlds. We have our home-life just like other people, but I should like to have a pony of my own, only I suppose my husband would not think it right to have a horse that was not a community-horse."

"What a confounded shame! I beg your pardon. You see I am rough. I mean, I think your husband ought to get you a pony, a nice well-trained lady's pony, for you to ride, and not a big farm-horse."

"I should like one," observed Olive simply, and then suddenly remembering that she was speaking to a stranger, she added hastily, "I mean it would be nice to have a horse always at hand, one not liable to be wanted for farm work."

"I just happen to know of an excellent animal that would suit you down to the ground. It belongs to Tom Mills, and he wants to sell it. It will go cheap too. If you would speak to your husband about it, I would bring it over for you to look at. Mills lives close to my house."

"No, pray don't," said Olive anxiously. "I am ever so much obliged to you, but I really ought not to have spoken about it."

"Very well," said he, seeing she was distressed, "we'll not pursue the subject further." But in his own mind he reflected that were he in Weston's place, he would have got that pony for his wife, principles or no principles, and it is highly probable that he would have done so.

He left Olive and her saddle at her own door, refusing her invitation to enter, saying that he would avail himself of her permission to come some other day to see her. And she cordially invited him to do so, for was not hospitality one of the commonest virtues of the prairie, and surely Perfection City must not be behindhand in the practice thereof?

# CHAPTER VIII.

### MR. PERSEUS.

WHEN Olive got home, she was at first pleased to see that her husband had not come in, therefore he had not been made uneasy about her absence. Napoleon Pompey had caught Rebel and turned him into the pasture field, and was returning after that job when he met Olive near the hen-house. Napoleon Pompey grinned at her and remarked with relish: "Ole hoss, he done throw yer, den run clar 'way home."

"No, he didn't," retorted Olive, indignant at this slur upon her equestrian skill, "I just got off to change the saddle, and he ran away from me."

"Land!" said Napoleon Pompey, "an' didn't yer chuck yer reins roun' yer arm?"

"No, I forgot to," confessed Olive.

"Golly Ned!" said Napoleon Pompey with vast amusement.

Olive felt annoyed and inquired stiffly where her husband was.

"Ole man he done gone ter git ole hoe men'd up, den he gwine ter go to der 'Sumbly, he done eat supper 'ready. Me an' you'uns got ter eat our'n now. Ole man done tol' me."

Napoleon Pompey meant no disrespect in speaking of Ezra as " ole man," for the lad knew of only two titles to bestow on white men, one was " Mas'r " the other was " ole man." Ezra had requested him not to use the expression Mas'r, which grated on his ears, and contained suggestions of servitude at variance with the ideas that prevailed at Perfection City. Napoleon Pompey was therefore obliged to fall back upon his one other title. Olive had been greatly shocked when she first heard her husband called " ole man," but she was now used to the expression.

She was very disappointed not to see Ezra at once, for she was full of her adventure, but she knew from experience she must possess her soul in patience, for the " 'Sumbly," as Napoleon Pompey called it, was sure to take a good while, and Ezra always stayed conscientiously to the last. The institution was none other than the bi-weekly Assembly, which met at the Academy, and at which all the business of the Community was settled and the routine work of the farm arranged for. All the members were free to attend and speak their minds, but in practice it had resolved itself into a Junta of Madame, Ezra, Wright, Green, and Uncle David, of whom the two latter were sleeping members. The women of Perfection City did not care to attend the Assembly very often. Women are not good debaters, and they dislike arguments carried on under strict rule. They prefer to go their own way, do what seems best at the moment, and reserve an unlimited right of grumbling and jealousy. Madame, who was an exception to the general rule, usually presided at the Assembly and ruled it, as she did most things, without seeming to do so. Ezra and Brother Wright understood the farm work and generally mapped out the daily labour pretty well. Brother Dummy required only to be told what to do and went on contentedly doing it, without comment or commotion. Nobody, of course, was ordered to work, but it was suggested that if Brother Wright would do so and so, Brother Ezra would be able to do this, that, or the other, while Brother Carpenter would be free to perform such another task, and Brother Dummy would probably prefer to work at whatever happened to be wanted at the moment. Madame seldom interfered, and then only when necessary to smooth over a rough edge. She usually found the men's arrangements excellent and for the general weal. Brother Green, who was a first-rate smith, was the only member of the Community who, at this time, received any money, for he worked in his spare time for outsiders. With great pride he used to bring the money he earned to the 'Sumbly and give it into Madame's charge to be expended as seemed best. She kept the accounts and used to furnish all the rest of the necessary cash. Sometimes the brethren expressed compunction at calling so often on her resources, but Madame always made the most graceful speeches in reply to their objections. Of course an undertaking such as this required capital to start it. It would be foolish to starve the whole project for want of a little expenditure now. By and by they would be self-supporting, but in order to reach that stage quickly they must not be stingy now. So she gave her dollars by the hundred when needed, and the brethren were eternally grateful and privately wondered if there was any limit to her wealth and generosity. At the Assembly it would be debated whether the next load of timber that was bought should go to building a hen-house for Brother Carpenter or to putting up a cattle-shed for Brother Ezra, and it speaks well for the honest conviction of the Pioneers that it was usually Brother Ezra who argued in favour of the hen-house, while Brother Carpenter expressed an anxious desire for the cattle-shed. The difficulty would perhaps be settled by Madame desiring to know how much timber was required for both buildings and deciding to buy that amount at the earliest opportunity.

At this particular Assembly to which we refer, Ezra was several times on the point of saying that he wished to get a pony for his wife, but his heart failed him. He knew he did want the pony very much, but he also knew that it was not really wanted for the Community. So he could not bring himself to give utterance to the individualistic wish, and after arranging the necessary business of the Community, he came home with his wish unstated.

Olive was waiting for him with the greatest impatience. She went, indeed, as far as the bars to meet him, but the road looked so lonesome and the sky so black with cold trembling specks of stars, that she ran back again in a flutter of panic to the house and shut herself in with the candles for company. At last he came back, and Olive poured forth the pent-up torrent of her news. Ezra was much amused at her description of the disaster and interested in her account of the rescuer.

"And I am so vexed," said Olive, "I can't for the life of me remember what he said his name was. I know I never heard it before, but he lives here on the prairie. It is so silly!"

"Call him Perseus," said Ezra laughing, "he was the gallant who came to the rescue of distressed damsels."

"What a good joke!" said Olive gleefully, "and I was a distressed damsel, I assure you. I cried with vexation."

"I have no doubt that Andromeda shed tears when she was bound to the rock," said Ezra, amused.

"And I was bound to that odious saddle by the bonds of duty," said Olive. "What a joke! Mr. Perseus!"

So they laughed and chatted, and Olive was as bright as possible, and Ezra thought again with a pang of that pony and almost wished he had spoken at the Assembly about it. Olive, however, never mentioned what Mr. Perseus had said about the pony Mills had for sale. The idea seemed to have passed from her mind.

It happened that about a week later Olive again found herself in the neighbourhood of Little Cotton Wood Creek, and by an extraordinary coincidence Mr. Perseus chanced to meet her. She was very much surprised, and he seemed to be no less so. However, the meeting was mutually pleasant, and they soon fell into conversation, as it appeared he was going her way.

"I have thought a great deal about what you said to me the other day, about trying to make life better and all that," said he with a certain self-consciousness, as if he was unaccustomed to speaking upon such a subject. Olive looked at him with bright clear eyes.

"I am very glad if anything I said could be of use to you, but I am myself very ignorant. I should like you to come and hear what Brother Wright says, and Ezra. Brother Wright is considered very eloquent. I can't always understand him myself, but that is my own deficiency!"

"I would much prefer talking with you, Mrs. Weston," said the stranger hastily. "I am very restive under men's teaching, but I am docile enough when led by a woman's gentle hand."

"Why are you living here?" asked Olive suddenly. "You seem so unsuited to this life."

"I am sick of civilization and all its horrors," said he. "I wanted to get away to something fresh and new."

"That is almost like what a Pioneer would say," remarked Olive with a smile. "They don't think very highly of what civilization has done so far."

"Materially it has done much, morally it has done badly for a good number of human beings," he remarked.

"I think you sound like a very hopeful convert to the principles of communism. Why don't you come to Perfection City?" asked Olive.

"Would you be glad to see me there, Mrs. Weston?"

"Certainly, Mr. Perseus, and I should be so pleased to make you and my husband known to each other."

He looked at her curiously for some moments and then said, "Why do you call me Mr. Perseus?"

Olive gave him one horrified glance and then blushed scarlet.

"Oh, I beg your pardon," she stammered in great confusion. "I did not know I said so. I really am most sorry."

"But why that name?" he persisted, still looking at her blushing face.

"I may as well tell you the truth," she said still much confused. "The fact is I forgot what you said your name was, and my husband suggested in a joke that I should call you Perseus, because—because——"

"I rescued you in distress," said he as he broke into a deep musical laugh. "It is a capital name, I am delighted with it."

"I am so ashamed of myself," said Olive, also laughing, "but I was in the habit of speaking of you as Mr. Perseus, and the name slipped off my tongue unawares. What is your real name? Pray tell me."

"Not for worlds, dear Mrs. Weston. To you I shall remain Mr. Perseus, and I shall never think of the name without a thrill of pleasure."

"But this is most unfair," said Olive. "You know my name and who I am and all about me, and yet I am to be kept in the dark as to your identity."

"Forgive my not doing at once what you wish, but really I cannot. This will be a sweet little innocent romance to me, and before you I shall appear in my very best light, leaving all the vices and evils of my real nature behind me for the time. Ah no! don't deprive me of such a harmless joy. If you knew what a lonely uncared for life is mine, your tender heart would be touched."

Her heart was touched by the quiver in his deep voice, as he intended it should be, and Olive did not press her point any further. They rode on together talking about a hundred subjects, and she found him the most agreeable of men. She happened to mention a great novel just then coming out in Harper's, the scene of which was laid in Florence, and he said musingly:

"Ah yes! Florence is a lovely city, nestling among the blue hills."

"Have you ever seen it then?" asked Olive much surprised.

"Yes, long ago, when I was a young fellow."

She gazed at him. "You are a most incomprehensible person," she said, "living here on this prairie and yet you have seen Florence."

"You forget Perseus travels easily with his winged feet, from here to Florence would be a bagatelle to him."

"I begin to think there must be something uncanny about you."

"Now don't go and change me into any other personality. Remember you are all-powerful, and by your word alone have made me Perseus. Your word is mighty, and you can cast me down into hell and make me a devil by a breath," said he half banteringly.

"What odd language!" said Olive, looking a little frightened. "How you must astonish the natives when you talk in that way!"

"Do you fancy I talk to anyone as I do to you? Don't you understand that I am Perseus to you, but to nobody else in the world?"

Olive laughed, and put her horse to a canter in order to snap the thread of talk which was becoming too difficult for her. Mr. Perseus remained in her company while she was driving home the cattle, but they had no further particular conversation, as the exigencies of driving the herd occupied their attention most of the time. On parting from her about a mile from her home, he promised to come some day to see her, and Olive added, "I do hope Ezra will be in, for I should so like you two to talk together. I am sure you have much in common."

"We have one point in common, at all events," thought Mr. Perseus as he rode away back towards the Big Cotton Wood Creek, "but I doubt very much if that would at all add to the harmony of our relations."

Olive was full of her meeting with Mr. Perseus, an account of which she retailed to Ezra at supper.

"And just fancy his oddity! He wouldn't tell me his real name after my unlucky slip, so he is Mr. Perseus to the end of the chapter, I suppose. He thought it such a joke."

"So he saw the application," remarked Ezra. "He must be a man of education."

"He is a most superior man, I can see that. He has read everything I ever did and more too. And do you know, Ezra, I shouldn't wonder if he had leanings towards community-life, many things he said pointed that way. Wouldn't it be funny if I were to be the one to bring in your first convert, poor little me that never had any leanings until I saw you."

Ezra looked sharply at his wife during this speech, for a sudden and by no means pleasant suspicion sprang into his mind concerning the mysterious Mr. Perseus. However, Olive looked so perfectly innocent of even all knowledge of evil that he felt ashamed of himself.

"I wouldn't be too friendly with this man. We don't know anything about him, nor who he is, remember," remarked Ezra.

"He said he knew you and that you were a fine-looking man, you old dear, and he is acquainted with most of the members of the Community by sight. Besides, I thought it was a point of etiquette on the prairie to make no inquiries into a person's character, but to take him in his boots just as he stands, and ask him to dinner. Don't you remember Charlie Clarke, and how he came to supper by your invitation and you found him so pleasant, and he a horse-thief and a murderer all the while, only we didn't know it."

This was all very true, but Charlie Clarke had evinced no "leanings" to community-life, and above all Olive had been profoundly uninterested in him and was delighted when he left. Ezra hated himself for the feeling in his heart, but he had his suspicions of Mr. Perseus, and he knew his wife was distractingly pretty. So he advised her to keep aloof from Mr. Perseus as much as practicable. Several times afterwards he made excuses to go riding with her, which Olive enjoyed immensely, but then something was said to her about his shirking his share of the work, and she was furiously angry. She wanted her husband to be first, and since the only theatre for the exhibition of his abilities was the somewhat restricted one of Perfection City, she wanted him to be always near the front.

"Shirking indeed!" she said tossing her pretty head. "I'll have Mary Winkle know my husband never shirked in his life."

In a blaze of wrath she met Ezra and ordered him to go to work and never mind riding with her till the harvest was over. She wouldn't ride any more, she would work until she was black in the face. Shirking indeed! She'd let Mary Winkle see! And so on and so forth, till her burst of anger had spent itself.

Olive was not slow to perceive that her husband had some sort of dislike to the idea of her seeing Mr. Perseus. She could not exactly explain to herself why this should be, and she was heartily sorry for it. She had fancied that in time Mr. Perseus might possibly come to be a member of the Community. She would indeed have been frankly glad to have him become a brother, for, as far as she could judge, he seemed a man of brilliant parts, and certainly his manners were most charming. To tell the truth, she found the members as a whole very uninteresting. Mary Winkle she positively disliked, and yet she was the one nearest to her own age. She sometimes wondered how Ezra could be satisfied with the companionship of those same people, who seemed to her to be walking in such a narrow circle, and always to be saying the same things in pretty nearly the same words. Now, Mr. Perseus said such original things and in such a charming voice. Altogether it was a pity that Ezra should have taken a prejudice into his head against this stranger. Olive wondered whether, if they met, the mutual recognition of their abilities would dissipate her husband's suspicions. Such being her notions, it was most unlucky that the first time Mr. Perseus came to see them Ezra should have been gone to Union Mills. He went so very seldom that it was a most unfortunate coincidence, as she explained to Mr. Perseus, who did not in return explain that having himself seen Ezra at Union Mills he had straightway ridden off to visit her, and ridden so hard too that his horse was in a white lather when he arrived at Perfection City by a somewhat circuitous route. Napoleon Pompey was gone, so Olive showed him where to put his horse in the dark stable so that the flies would not torment the animal. She remarked on the horse's state and asked Mr. Perseus had he been running down cattle, and he muttered something about young horses showing every bit of work in hot weather.

He was profoundly interested in Olive's little home. She showed him with pride the garden she had made, where already the balsams were just coming into blossom; she then took him to see the prairie chickens she was trying to rear, little black and yellow downy things, with fierce wild eyes utterly untamed and only looking out for a favourable opportunity to make a dash for freedom.

"Do you think I can ever tame them?" asked Olive, as she noted the hostile manner in which they scuttled away from her food-giving hand.

"If anyone could tame them you could, the ungrateful little brutes!" remarked Mr. Perseus.

"I don't see that it is ungrateful of them to resent being taken from their proper home and natural mother to be put under a fat stupid hen," said Olive.

"No, but it is rank ingratitude not to be tame to you," said he.

"I don't think you are truthful," said Olive bluntly.

"Why?" asked Mr. Perseus.

"Because you are always saying things like that," she answered, somewhat resentfully.

"Well, I do call that hard," complained Mr. Perseus, "to charge a fellow with being untruthful when he was shaking in his shoes from terror at having perhaps let out too much of the truth."

Olive looked down at his big boots, knitting her brows, and then led the way into the house.

"I'll get you some dinner. I am sure you are hungry," she said hospitably, it being about two o'clock in the afternoon.

"I am hungry, starving, mind, body, and soul," said her visitor in reply.

"I'll get a chicken-pie for you, that will go some way," answered Olive with a laugh.

"And if you will talk with me, that will go far to complete the work of charity," said he.

Olive brought him the food, and he set to work upon it, being evidently, as he said, very hungry.

"Do you know I am beginning to look upon Perfection City as a sort of earthly paradise," said Mr. Perseus.

"Indeed."

"Yes, a paradise from which I am shut out. Have you any young men here, Mrs. Weston, unmarried men, or are they against your rules?"

"No. Unmarried men are not against our rules," said Olive archly. "We had one here lately, but we haven't now."

"Why, what did you do with him?" asked Mr. Perseus, in some surprise.

"I married him," said Olive dimpling and blushing.

"Lucky beggar!" remarked her visitor, turning again to his dinner.

Mr. Perseus stayed some time, but refused Olive's invitation to wait to see her husband, saying as an excuse that he had a long way to ride home. Olive wanted to know where he lived, but he laughingly put her off. He would not tell her, lest she should discover his real name, and then much of the romance of his life would be destroyed.

"You don't know what this is to me, and how when I am leading my lonely life, I recall every word and look and again go through these meetings, Mrs. Weston. I suppose it seems silly to you, but remember, human companionship is man's most precious inheritance, and those who have but little of it prize what they have at perhaps an extravagant figure. Did you ever hear of Silvio Pellico?" he asked abruptly.

"No," replied Olive.

"Well, he was a prisoner entirely shut off from human companionship, and he at last made friends with a spider, and at length the spider was crushed by the turnkey's foot, and Silvio wept tears of anguish. I am like a prisoner out here on this desolate prairie."

"And am I like the horrible spider, then?" said Olive brightly.

"Mrs. Weston!" he exclaimed reproachfully. "I have opened my heart to you because I felt that you could feel with me, although the world might count us as strangers, but I thought you would understand what I meant even when I blundered through the expression of my thoughts. This is the first time you have misunderstood me. But I believe it was only pretended misunderstanding and that you do know what I meant."

He said good-bye, and left Olive with a feeling of sadness and oppression on her mind. He had not been as bright as before, and she wondered who he was and why he was so anxious not to see anyone but her. She mentioned his visit to Ezra, but somehow she had less to tell about him than on former occasions. There seemed nothing to say. Ezra, too, did not appear as much amused as formerly at the joke of Mr. Perseus. No doubt it was getting stale by this time.

## CHAPTER IX.

### FIRST LESSONS.

Summer came on apace. The field had been duly run over in both directions with the shovel-plough, so as to leave between the cross-ploughing little "hills" of earth, out of which sprang the corn-clumps. The broad green ribbons of leaves fluttered in the wind, making a soft murmur as of a forest. Olive took great delight in her little flower-garden at the east end of the house, and worked and weeded at it both early and late. Napoleon Pompey, typical negro boy, which being interpreted means laziest of mortals, forgot his laziness to work for "Mis' Ollie" as he called her. Together they had planted their balsams, trained their morning-glory, and rooted out brown beetles with zeal, to be amply repaid in July by a glorious profusion of blossoms.

"This is my very ownest own garden," said Olive, exhibiting her balsams with pride to Ezra. "Mind, this is not community-land, it's mine."

"Does it make you enjoy the flowers more to think that nobody else has them?" asked Ezra, with a tinge of sadness in his voice. "Would it make you any the happier to keep the sunshine all to yourself, do you think?"

"No, certainly not, that's quite different. But I've planted these flowers and grown them. I shall give them to whomsoever I like. You for instance." She smiled coaxingly at him.

"You pretty child," he said, disarmed.

"Why, I brought some over to Mrs. Carpenter to-day. I went to help her with her washing. And, do you know!" said Olive, "I was so amused."

"At what?"

"Mr. Carpenter was educating his children."

"He's always doing that," said Ezra.

"Yes, but to-day there was a special lesson. He was at Union Mills yesterday, and he got a present for both of them, I mean two presents, one for Johnny and one for Nelly. You know he is always saying boys and girls would have the same tastes if they were brought up in the same way."

"He'll find out one day, maybe, that boys will be boys, no matter how you bring them up."

"He has found it out already. Wait till you hear. By way of correcting any early bias, he gave a hammer and nails to Nelly and a doll to Johnny."

"You don't say so! What did the children do?"

"Well, they went off without a word, each carrying its toy, and Mr. Carpenter told me his ideas about education, and how well they worked. Suddenly we heard shrieks from behind the wood-pile where the children were playing. We ran out to see what was the matter. Nelly had got a handkerchief tied over the head of her hammer, and she was cuddling it to sleep in her arms. Johnny had got some of the nails and was trying to drive them into a piece of wood with the head of the doll for hammer. Nelly was screaming because he was killing poor Dolly."

Ezra laughed, and Olive joined in at the recollection of the scene. "You cannot think how disappointed Mr. Carpenter looked. His wife said he'd got something to do if he was expecting to cure little girls of dolls in a hurry. We changed the presents and left him to reconcile it with his theories as best he could; both children were quite happy and contented afterwards."

"Poor Carpenter! He'll have to learn by bitter experience that he cannot change human nature all at once," said Ezra, sympathetically. "I fear children are still in the savage stage of development, they are not communists."

"Nobody is communist about things they care very much about," said Olive, in desperate courage.

"Why, Ollie! What a thing to say! I am a thorough-going communist I hope. I'd give the coat off my back without a pang."

"Of course you would, because it is a horrid old thing any way, and men look frights in coats always. Men don't care about clothes, only just to cover themselves and keep themselves warm. One rag would do as well as another."

"You are an incorrigible little individualist and a greedy one as well, I do declare," said Ezra, half laughing at her vehemence.

"No, it's not that, only I see what is what," replied Olive oracularly.

"And what might that be?"

"The Pioneers are only communistic for rubbish and rags, and not for dolls and hammers. That's what they are," said Olive, with her face aflame.

"Rubbish and rags! What an absurd thing to say. Who ever heard such nonsense?" said Ezra, loftily ignoring his wife's argument in a way that wise men often affect.

"'Tisn't nonsense," said Olive hotly. "It is just what people say of Perfection City."

"What people say it?" asked Ezra.

"Well, Mr. Perseus for one," said Olive, repenting of her daring in getting into the subject at all.

"Mr. Perseus," repeated Ezra with a sudden frown, "so you talk over our principles with him. When did you do so last?"

"I don't know exactly when. The other day. He often passes by here on his way cattle-hunting. Sometimes he looks in for a moment, but sometimes he can't stay long, only to water his horse. Of course I talk over the principles that have made you found a City here. Don't you suppose people know about them and talk them over eagerly? They are different enough from the generality of people's ideas, and Mr. Perseus said they considered you only went a little way into communism, and had a little bit of this and a little bit of that in common, and weren't at all logical. People sneer at Perfection City, I can assure you."

"And you, doubtless, enjoyed his sneers," retorted Ezra injudiciously.

"No, I didn't, only I saw what other people say of us. Mr. Perseus, even, once said he'd like to come and be a communist himself, if we were only consistent throughout, and lived up to our principles."

"You may tell your friend Perseus that he would not be a welcome recruit," said Ezra, in considerable agitation. "I may as well tell you now what I have suspected for some time. I know pretty well who your mysterious Mr. Perseus is. He is a man of the name of Cotterell. I know him very well by sight and better still by reputation. To convince you, I will just mention a point or two about his appearance. He is about five feet ten in height, very fair in complexion, with a yellow moustache, and bright blue eyes, and whenever he takes his hat off you see the blue veins very markedly on his temples. He is, I suppose, what a woman would call a very handsome man, and he usually rides a black horse with a blaze on his face and white hind feet."

"Yes, that's the man," said Olive who remembered

the horse well, and who moreover recognized the perfect accuracy of her husband's description.

"Very well. Now I will tell you something about his character and history. He is an Englishman and perhaps has been badly brought up. At all events he hasn't the morals we approve of. I know his libertine London ways. He probably didn't tell you about it, but I remember very well the poor girl who shot herself the first summer we came here, because Cotterell had abandoned her. If the neighbours had been quite sure of all the facts of the case, there would in all probability have been a shooting party at Cotterell's house, so I was told. But they were not quite sure so they gave him the benefit of the doubt. Accordingly he still has his handsome face to go on with and maybe wreck more homes. That is the career of Mr. Cotterell, alias Mr. Perseus," said Ezra with considerable heat.

"It was you who gave him the name of Perseus," replied Olive also much agitated. "He did not appear under a false name of his own accord. And now that you tell me his real name I remember that was the one he gave the first time I saw him, and he asked me if I had ever heard it before."

"I won't say anything on that point, it may have been a joke on his part, but it must stop now. Understand me, Olive. I don't wish to seem harsh, but you must not meet and talk with this man again. If you chance on him, pass by and say you can have no further communication with him. If he urges an objection, say I have forbidden you to see him, as I do forbid you, here and now. He will take that for an answer, scoundrel as he is, for among people of his stamp personal vanity does duty for better feelings. He won't come again to a house where the lady has once shown him the door. You don't in the least understand what his motives are in this new-fangled interest of his in Perfection City, but I understand them very clearly, and my wish is that you never see him again. Harm is sure to come of it if you do."

Olive was very much alarmed at her husband's stern manner and peremptory order, but she was also indignant. Mr. Perseus or Cotterell, as she must now call him, had shown great respect and deference to her and had evinced a desire to be guided by her to higher aspirations. She was not sure of the meaning of some of his remarks, or rather she wished she could find some other reasonable explanation for them than the one most people would undoubtedly attach to them. Still she resented her husband's masterful manner.

"I will of course obey your orders, Ezra," she said with a tart emphasis on the word which made him wince, "because I hold old-fashioned ideas of what wifely duty is, quite at variance with the high standard of individual liberty as maintained and explained, I believe, by the brethren of Perfection City. You may rest quite satisfied, I will obey you."

Having thus stabbed her husband in his most vulnerable point and dexterously driven the poignard up to the hilt in the wound, Olive walked away, leaving Ezra to feel himself a selfish brute.

Ezra spent a wretched half-day of self-reproach, and then crept back repentant, begging to be forgiven for being a tyrant to his poor little pet. And his little pet who had paid for her pride with abundant tears, allowed him to kiss her and fondle her and call her sweet silly names, while she declared she never cared to see or speak to that wretched Mr. Cotterell again, and no wonder he was ashamed of his own name, etc., etc., all in the most foolish and approved manner possible to the newly married.

All the same, after a time Olive began to feel sorry for Mr. Cotterell, and to pity him for the very errors of his past life, about which she now saw that he was penitent without wishing to explain to her why. Also she had very much enjoyed meeting him; he was so fresh, cultivated, and original, in his conversation. It was really very dull sometimes with no one to talk to, and the long hot day shimmering by, making her feel as if she were a potato being slowly baked in a hot-air oven. There was no excitement in the house-work and—and it was very dreary sometimes. Men delight in reverting to primitive savagery. The most highly civilized man "reverts" in a way which is surprising both for completeness and for rapidity, but women hate the process. Savage woman was a slave, and the more completely a woman becomes subject to primitive conditions the more closely she resembles a slave, and is in virtual bondage either to some human being or to hampering circumstances.

Of appropriate companions of her own sex Olive had absolutely none. Mary Winkle was a rigid reformer, a person all angles, of the sort that never becomes a companion to anyone, for she was always on the war-path, and, besides, between her and Olive there was an unexpressed, but no less real, antipathy. Her daughter, Willette, that creature half boy, half girl, and wholly wild, was always on horseback careering after stray cattle, and though by her ignorance and eccentricity she sometimes amused Olive, she had really no ideas beyond those very concrete ones impressed upon her from without by her open-air life on the prairie. Mrs. Carpenter was a good soul, but a mere stout housewife, with no ideas and only one hope, namely, "that Carpenter would give up his highfallutin' notions, an' go back to York State, an' settle down comfortable again, an' be a preacher in a Baptist church." Mrs. Ruby was old in body, but the youngest of them all in mind, except Uncle David, who was her senior by four years. Mrs. Ruby believed in Perfection City, though she reserved the right of private judgment on certain of the tenets of its founders, and in particular, she had lately felt misgivings as to the worldly wisdom of their principle of non-resistance. She knew, however, that the Pioneers were going to show the world the new and better way—the way which led into no competition for supremacy, but into peaceful paths of universal progress. Property and its attendant imps, greed, strife, jealousy, envy, hatred, and malice, were all banished from Perfection City, and in their place peace and good-will and perfect trust in each other were to reign forever. It was a high ideal, but not a new one. It was eighteen centuries old, though it had never yet been realised. Mrs. Ruby and Uncle David felt sure they had reached the ideal, and all through Madame Morozoff-Smith, the most whole-souled, unselfish, glorious woman of her century. It was a pity she had not a larger theatre in which to present before mankind the new principles of social life it was their privilege to put into practice.

## CHAPTER X.

### PRACTICAL COMMUNISM.

A DAY or two after Ezra had laid his commands upon his wife, as we saw in the last chapter, he came home in the evening to find her in floods of tears. Her eyelids were all red with weeping, and she broke out afresh on seeing him.

"What's the matter?" asked Ezra, in much concern. "What has happened?"

"My poor flowers, my pretty balsams!" sobbed Olive.

"Has the calf got into your garden and spoiled your flowers, my poor child?" he said tenderly.

"No, it wasn't the calf, but they are all gone. Mary Winkle took them all."

"Oh!" said Ezra with a slight shock of surprise.

"Yes, she has cleared the whole garden. She came to-day while I was out at Mrs. Huntley's."

"How do you know it is she who has taken them?"

"Napoleon Pompey told me he saw her pick them."

"Depend upon it, he is lying," said Ezra with

emphasis. "Negroes are as mischievous as monkeys, and——"

"No, he didn't do anything to the flowers," interrupted Olive. "He was as pleased with them almost as I was myself, and worked ever so hard to help keep down the weeds. Besides, I went to Mary Winkle and saw them."

"Oh!" said Ezra helplessly. He wished it had been the calf or Napoleon Pompey or anybody or anything rather than Mary Winkle. He braced himself for what was coming.

"She told me she did it with a purpose. She said I was getting more individualistic in my leanings every day, and that time was not curing me at all, that I was selfishly proud of my flowers. It isn't one bit true," sobbed Olive, with quivering chin. "I gave heaps of them away. I gathered a bunch for Mrs. Huntley just as I was going this morning."

Ezra groaned. "I know you did, dear," he said.

"She said I gloated over them and rejoiced because nobody else had any. I didn't. I only loved them because I had tended them and reared them, and I knew them and watched for their buds. She said they didn't belong to me, but to the Community, and that she took them on behalf of the general weal. Those are all grand words for nasty mean jealousy and covetousness," said Olive passionately. "I hate Mary Winkle and I hate the Community."

"Oh, Olive, Olive!" cried Ezra with a gesture of

entreaty. "Don't say that, dear. It strikes me to the heart. Think of me, dear."

"My pretty flowers!" she said with a drooping of her mouth that betokened fresh tears.

"I am so sorry, oh, more sorry than I can say," said Ezra. "Mary Winkle has done wrong, and has administered a lesson in a cruel, brutal way."

"She has no business to give me lessons at all, and I won't take them from her," cried Olive passionately. "I hate being the one to be always taught. They think themselves so superior and are always stooping to raise me. Let them raise themselves first. I can see where Mary Winkle needs teaching and correction as plainly as anybody. She is only communistic in regard to things she doesn't really care about."

"No, no Ollie, darling. It is really a deep conviction with us all, although in this case most unkindly illustrated," said Ezra gently.

"I know you think so in all honesty, but it isn't so in reality. Nobody is nor can be communistic about what they love, if it is real love. If they are communistic about a thing it is because they don't really care."

Ezra knew by the pang of jealousy in his own heart that this was an insurmountable truth his little wife was hurling forth in her anger.

"Mary Winkle isn't communistic. I'm not clever and able to say wise things and use long words that amaze people like Brother Wright, but for all that I can see some things clearly enough. Mary Winkle isn't any more communistic than I am, only we love different things."

"I think you mistake," said Ezra.

"No, I don't mistake one bit. Let Mary Winkle, if she is communistic in all the moods and tenses, lump her child with the two little Carpenters and draw lots to take one of the three for her own. Would that satisfy her heart, although the precious principles would be right enough? Of course not, because her heart would step in and claim its own by the divine right of love. I should be thoroughly communistic on the score of these children. I shouldn't mind to draw lots as to whether Willette or Nelly or Johnny Carpenter was going to come to live with me. One would do as well as another, and I could be thoroughly communistic, because I don't love any of them very deeply. My little flowers I did love. It wasn't that I had worked for them and grudged the fruit of my labour. I would work in a turnip field and let anyone who liked have the turnips, nasty, watery, pulpy things, but I loved those flowers and tended them and they were mine. I don't care about the philosophy of the question. You will perhaps some day see what I mean, Ezra, and understand me. I know you don't now. You think me a silly child."

In his own heart he thought he understood more clearly than he liked to confess, that Olive was speaking more than philosophy, she was announcing stubborn facts. However, he strove his utmost to soothe her feelings, for he could see that if an attitude of strife and hostility were once set up between her and Mary Winkle, it would not only affect his wife's happiness but might have very serious results upon the future of Perfection City. There were only a very few of them, and if the experiment was to succeed it could only do so through unity, while strife and internal dissensions would certainly destroy it without giving it a chance. This point was fruitful of deep meditation, and occasioned heart-searchings to Ezra. It indeed augured ill for the future, not only of Perfection City, but of all those other cities of their imagination which should spring from this mother plant, if the personal feelings of a couple of good women were potent enough to wreck the scheme. Surely, in the dozen or so choice spirits who now formed the entire population of that City, there could be none of those latent forces making for destruction which would have to be reckoned with in the future and larger experiments in communism they were leading up to. If it was so difficult to soothe ruffled feelings in Perfection City now, and to compose a quarrel about some wretched little balsams, what would happen when, in a larger Perfection City, deeper cause of dispute arose between numbers of persons? Ezra's mind recoiled aghast at the answer which rose up in his mind in reply to that question. There would have to be some strong, some overwhelming central power, a despot in short. Was this then the goal which they were to reach after toiling along a hard and stony road of personal effort? A despotism or a monasticism, in either case tyranny and subjection. Surely, oh surely, there must be some other solution which his mind, disturbed by the sight of his little wife's distress, had unaccountably failed to formulate. He would go to Madame and would seek guidance from her illumined mind.

Olive, spent by her emotions, had gone to sleep quite early, so Ezra sallied forth to seek counsel where he was used to find it. Madame would be sure to be still up—though it was late by prairie hours, after nine o'clock—as he knew by experience, for in his bachelor days he had often spent long evenings in discussion and talk with her. Since his marriage, however, he had never gone alone in the evening to talk with Madame. Happy in his own love, he had felt no need of other companionship, and now as he walked along to her house, he began to wonder if she had noticed the sudden cessation of the evening talks, and also to wonder if she had missed them. It was thoughtless never to have gone near her during all these weeks. It was selfish, seeing how kind, how always sympathetic she had been to him for so many months, during the time when he felt lonely and full of undefined longings, before his heart had found complete rest in Olive's love and above all in his love for her. Ezra thinking of these things was smitten with remorse, and made a resolution to go and see Madame of an evening sometimes and to bring Olive with him. Meantime he walked along and in a few moments knocked at the familiar door. Madame opened it herself, with Balthasar in close attendance. The latter, on satisfying himself that it was a person of friendly intentions who claimed admittance, walked back to the spot where he had been lying, and resumed the thread of his interrupted slumbers.

"Brother Ezra, this is indeed a most unexpected visit. I hope it is not because there is anything wrong in your little home," said Madame gravely.

Ezra felt much embarrassed. He could hardly say there was nothing the matter, and still less could he apologise for having forgotten during all these happy weeks to come to see her. He did the best thing under the circumstances. He ignored Madame's remark and question, and plunged boldly into the business which had brought him.

She listened gravely without making any observation, but occasionally the faintest shadow of a smile fluttered around her lips. Ezra watched her face somewhat anxiously. In the old days, he had been used to read her face when they talked together, and to catch the meaning of her words from the mobile and ever-changing expression of her clear blue eyes. But to-day, somehow, as he looked, he felt he had lost the power to read. The face was now a mask which seemed to conceal the real woman underneath, and yet it was the same fair smooth brow, the same sharply defined eyebrows, and, beneath, the same eyes. No, the eyes were not the same. They no longer looked clear and full at Ezra, but were often averted in a strange and uncertain manner, as if seeking to hide or to flee. At least such was the curious impression they produced upon him, as he sat looking at her and telling of the mighty wave of wrath that had surged up about that handful of balsam blossoms.

"It is a most singular cause of division, and one I could almost laugh at, except for the very real passions of anger and of hatred it has aroused," he said in conclusion.

"One often sees terrible bursts of anger and fury in immature minds," observed Madame in the preamble of her answer. "Young children and people of weak intellect frequently exhibit the most pitiable extremes of fury over trifling causes."

Ezra was not quite certain to what she referred. If to Olive, then she was mistaken in considering her a child. He recalled very vividly what she had said about communism in what one loves, and he was not at all prepared to admit that her arguments were those of a person of weak intellect.

"I don't think this is a case for 'criticism-cure' in the Assembly, do you?" she said.

"No, certainly not," replied Ezra, who was keenly alive to the possibility of his wife's blazing up into uncompromising criticism herself, if they attempted to apply the famous "cure" upon her.

"Criticism-cure" existed rather in theory than in practice in Perfection City, but it was held that if a brother or a sister should be guilty of any offence against the common weal, it would be an edifying experience to summon him or her to the Assembly, and let all the members tell him or her exactly what each one thought of the conduct in question. In theory this was supposed to work admirably, and to be a weapon capable of reducing to reason the most refractory member of the Community, but when Ezra remembered it and imagined for a moment its possible effects on Olive, he foresaw a whole train of deplorable results. Suppose she defended herself, she could say sharp rankling things with a surprising amount of unanswerable truth in them, or suppose she didn't defend herself, but took the scolding silently. Her eyes would get bigger and bigger with tears which would roll over her cheeks, and her sweet little chin would quiver, and she would look imploringly at him. He couldn't stand that, he knew, but would rush up and take her in his arms, and carry her off out from the midst of the carping, criticising brethren, and he would call her sweet pet and darling, and say she was right and they were horrid brutes to scold her, and he would be very angry and would be quite capable of knocking Brother Wright down, if he, as was likely, had been savage with the little pet. No, criticism-cure should not be applied to Olive. And Ezra, arguing thence into wider fields, began to feel some doubts as to the value of that remarkable weapon as a means of eradicating the naturally evil tendencies of the human heart. Theories which had seemed sound and complete in the abstract had a curious habit of ringing false when he imagined himself as applying them to Olive. It was very curious, but they did not seem to fit her, or was it possible that the theories themselves were wrong? No, he dismissed that thought as entailing too much mental demolition and carting away of rubbish. Of one thing only was he sure, the "criticism-cure" was not to be tried on his little wife.

"I think it is a case for petting rather than for punishing," remarked Madame, after an interval during which they had both been severally following out the ramifications of their own reflections.

Ezra jumper at this idea. He was of that opinion too, as he impartially observed. Indeed he was always of opinion that Olive required petting.

"Yes, I think I understand the case," continued Madame. "The flowers were a toy, doubly prized now they are gone. What is wanted is to provide a new and more attractive toy, so that the baby-mind will lightly forget the old grief."

Ezra did not quite like this way of referring to Olive, but he had called in Madame's aid, and he had no choice but to listen to the physician's diagnosis and prescription regarding the case in question. Madame meanwhile looked at him half pityingly, having apparently overcome her eyes' desire to avoid his glance.

"Poor Ezra!" she said softly. "You are mated to a child, petulant, wilful, hard to manage, and very bewitching. You will find that you cannot in this case work by the light of pure reason. You must bring yourself down to her level and try to see with her eyes, to take delight in the petty trifles that interest her. 'Tis weary work! The task of Sisyphus was none the less severe because it produced no tangible good."

She was silent, and Ezra began to repent that he had sought counsel from so exalted a source, since it was delivered to him with such a liberal seasoning of the bitter salt of implied reproof.

"I think that I can apply a remedy in this instance," resumed Madame. "I know a woman's mind as well as most people, and I know too the vain weaknesses of a silly girl—perhaps the knowledge comes from a memory, or perhaps from a shattered hope, who knows? At all events, dear friend and brother, it will serve you now."

She left him to go into the small inner apartment which was her bedroom, and came out again in a few moments carrying a small gold bracelet of curious workmanship, an Oriental trinket.

"Here is a little trifle I happen to have by me. Do you think this toy would dry the little one's tears?"

She handed the bracelet to Ezra, who, though ignorant enough on such matters, did not fail to recognise the flash of diamonds in the jewel.

"This is a very valuable piece of jewellery," he said. "You must not give it away."

"I don't value such things except for the power of making someone happy," replied Madame. "Take it, dear friend, and think that I speak truly when I say I would gladly give all I possess to ease your mind of trouble and make your path in life a pleasant one. And the child-wife may like it. Now, go to her. Goodnight! You look tired and harassed."

She gently put her hand upon his forehead as if to smooth out wrinkles, and left the room.

As Ezra walked home with the diamond bracelet in his pocket, he seemed to feel her cool soft touch still, and the thought came into his mind that Olive never petted him. No, it was he who always petted her. Well, she was very sweet and pretty, and he hoped the bracelet would comfort her.

There was no doubt about that. Olive danced for joy when she saw the trinket. She put it on her smooth little wrist and flashed it about in the sunshine. Her eyes rivalled the diamonds for brightness.

"Do you like it, Ollie?"

"Like it! Why, it's too lovely for anything, and Madame is just a darling, and she is kind. Just fancy giving me a diamond bracelet! A thing I never dreamt of ever owning. And how shall I ever thank her?"

Olive was skipping with joy. Suddenly she stopped short.

"Ezra, is this mine, or is it a community-bracelet?"

"It is yours, child."

"Mary Winkle can't come and take it away for the good of my soul, can she?"

"No, certainly not. We are allowed to hold private property in such personal trifles, as you know quite well. Besides, Sister Mary would not wish to take from you what you particularly prized."

"Oh, of that I am not at all so sure. If your principles allowed it, I would not give much for Sister Mary's self-restraint in the matter. She might want the bracelet for herself or for Willette, for what I know. I shall tell her the bracelet is mine even by community-law."

Olive began to skip again.

"You are an intractable little mortal, for all you look so soft and yielding," said Ezra. He could not help smiling at her pretty kittenish ways, but he was filled with a sort of amazement to perceive how impossible it was to change the trend of her mind. Had she been an angular woman, all bones, like Mary Winkle, it would not have seemed so strange. Olive brought her frollicking to a conclusion and looked wisely at her husband, shaking her pretty little head at him.

"No, no, Ezra. It is not that, but you are trying to stuff me into a wrong-shaped mould, and I don't fit. As if any mortal woman ever could care for a community-bracelet!"

She danced away to put her treasure in some safe place, and Ezra went off to his work, wondering in his own mind if there was something radically antagonistic to communism in the female nature. If there was any such fundamental incompatibility of temperament, then farewell to all ideas of a successful issue to their experiment. Absolute equality between men and women in position, power, and influence was the key-note of their theories, but what would become of these theories if it should appear that the female mind refused to accept the first and greatest postulate upon which they were all founded?

# CHAPTER XI.

### A CHANCE MEETING.

The spring whence the Westons drew their water was about a quarter of a mile from the house across an angle of the corn field. A little foot-path winding in and out among the hills of corn led to it. As the corn grew, this path changed in character and became at length a track through a miniature forest. The corn grew to about eight feet in height, and of course the first to be covered was little Olive, with her brief five feet two inches, but by the end of July it had covered them all. Then it became Olive's greatest delight to go down through that forest where the corn shook in the breeze. The satin-smooth stalks coming up like bamboos, and the broad fibrous ribbons of leaves, were a constant pleasure. But greatest joy of all was to watch the coming of the silk. When the young ears of grain were forming they threw off great skeins of exquisite silken threads, changing through every tint from palest green to rich dark crimson. These bunches of silk were like soft plumes falling from the crest of the husk that held the ears, and were most tempting to twist through idle fingers. A forest of tall-growing prairie corn is just the place for fairies, only alas! the wee folk had departed this life long before ever Olive went to live at Perfection City. So charmed was she with this dwarf forest, which afforded the only shade to be enjoyed on that glaring prairie, that during the summer she always went to the spring for an extra pail of fresh water every afternoon before supper-time, as this errand gave her an excuse for loitering among the corn stalks and amusing herself with her own playful fancies.

Diana of course accompanied her young mistress upon these walks to the spring, for the puppy was attached to her by bonds of firmest canine affection, while Olive, on her side, was never tired of laughing at Diana's ridiculous freaks, although they sometimes caused her considerable trouble.

Take an example.

A day so hot and scorching that words fail to convey any idea of it, and Olive in a great fuss, for she was behindhand with her work. At four o'clock, the very most blistering hour of the whole twenty-four, she set off hastily for the spring to fetch the fresh water, and with her Diana, her tongue lolling out half a hand's breath. Knowing the object of the expedition, the puppy took the path through the corn, and Olive sweltered after her. It seemed as if the shelter of the corn was powerless against the slanting shafts of sunlight that danced and chequered between the broad hanging leaves, while the very air seemed endowed with such a load of heat as to press down with more than the allotted weight upon Olive's head. She climbed over the fence and walked across the grass to where the spring started from under a tiny overhanging ledge of limestone rock. It was an excellent spring with the best of water, and would have been made into the holiest of wells by a spreading tree or a shady thorn-bush near it. There was, however, nothing of this sort, but only a clear pool of water some two feet across and about a foot deep, just enough, in fact, to enable one to get a good dip with the bucket. As Olive, hot and tired, hurried to this little pool of water, she beheld the accomplished Diana sitting in the middle of it, cooling herself and slobbering water up and down over her nose in supreme bliss. Poor Olive! She did not know whether to laugh or to cry, but eventually decided upon the first-named course. Then she sat down beside Diana and paddled her feet in the water, after which refreshment she returned home with her water-pail empty. The spring had an undisturbed night in which to renew its freshness, and in the future Olive kept her eye on Diana when they went together for water. The dog always wanted to go first, but Olive kept her severely to heel until the water was obtained, after which Diana was free to indulge in what diversions she pleased.

One day as Olive emerged from the pathway through the corn, her heart gave a great bound of alarm as she saw a man standing beside the spring, holding his horse's bridle. He was a tall man in a red shirt and large-brimmed hat. He carried a revolver at his belt, but it was not that which frightened Olive, she was well accustomed to seeing armed men. On catching sight of her the stranger took off his hat with a sweeping bow, and coming forward greeted her with the greatest eagerness.

"This is indeed a delightful meeting, Mrs. Weston. Quite idyllic, if I may say so. And are you coming to fetch water? It is a subject for a poem, only I am not a poet. I can feel all the beauty of it, but must be dumb. You'll let me carry back your pail for you, won't you? It is too heavy for those wee hands."

"Thank you, Mr. Cotterell. I can quite easily carry my pail. I do it every day," said Olive speaking with much embarrassment.

"Mr. Cotterell!" he repeated with infinite sadness in manner, and with a look of much meaning in his bold blue eyes. "You call me Mr. Cotterell, then I am no longer Mr. Perseus, and my sweet romance is shattered forever!"

"I know now that you are Mr. Cotterell," said Olive, in keen distress.

"And knowing that, you are disillusioned and have lost faith in me, and you will not even let me carry your pail of water for you," said he, sadly, in a way which cut Olive to the heart, " yet I am the same man I was. To you at least I have never changed."

" I know you are very kind," said Olive, " but if you please I'd rather you didn't carry the pail for me."

She was dreadfully sorry to say anything to hurt his feelings, but she remembered her promise, and she must make him understand here and now that their acquaintance was to cease. She wanted to do it as kindly as she could, but she must do it at once.

Cotterell was not slow to read her thoughts, indeed her distress was too real and undisguised for him to fail to understand.

" Is this an order of dismissal, Mrs. Weston? Am I not to come to see you any more? " he asked abruptly, with a look of pain in his face.

Olive glancing up saw the pain and felt sorrier than ever, but she went bravely forward.

" I am deeply pained, Mr. Cotterell, but I must ask you not to come to see me; my husband does not want you to," she said, unable in her distress to find any words which would convey her meaning unmistakably, and yet not sound too unkind.

" Your husband has forbidden you to see me? " said Cotterell, biting his yellow moustache savagely.

" Yes," said Olive simply.

" Your husband's sentiments would do credit to a dog in the manger, Mrs. Weston, but are not what one exactly looks for from a professing communist, who poses as a shining light for his poor fellow-creatures still groping in the darkness of their ignorance."

"He says you are a bad man, Mr. Cotterell," said Olive with a view to defending her husband and perhaps finding out the facts of the case about her mysterious friend, in whose personality she felt a great interest.

"I don't pretend to be a good man, Heaven knows! but I'm a poor lonely devil living quite by myself, and your husband, with all that the world can give in the way of happiness, grudges me the brief pleasure of talking for half an hour with a good woman. That's not the way to make me a better man, Mrs. Weston, and God knows I need all the help I can get."

"I'm so sorry," faltered Olive in ready sympathy, and the tears welled up into her tender black eyes.

"You sweet pitying angel," said Mr. Cotterell, coming nearer and speaking very gently. "Your influence would save me if anything could."

"Oh, you mustn't talk like that," said Olive, with a catch in her voice. "And you will be a good man, won't you?"

He bent his handsome face low, and taking her hand implanted a kiss upon it with a grace that might have charmed a duchess.

"A woman can make or mar a man's life," said he. "Happy are they who draw the prizes. Good-bye!"

He sprang upon his horse and galloped away. Olive stood watching him, her eyes swimming in tears, she scarcely knew why, only he seemed so sad and so handsome. Ezra was unkind to say she must never see him any more and try to make his life less sad and wicked, and she was so sorry to think that she would never have any more talks with him.

At this moment a low growl from Diana made Olive turn round to encounter the clear cool gaze of Madame Morozoff-Smith.

"I followed you down here," she said. "Napoleon Pompey told me that you were most likely gone to the spring."

"Have you been here long?" asked Olive, blushing in her surprise and confusion. "I only came for a pail of fresh water."

"No, I just saw Mr. Cotterell say good-bye and ride off," observed Madame gently. "Do you see him often? He hasn't a good reputation."

"I don't believe he is as bad as people say, I am very sorry for him living alone."

"He need not have been alone only that he chose it, indeed it ought to have been quite otherwise, if report goes true."

"We ought to be the last persons on earth to credit reports," said Olive hotly. "I am sure there is a nice crop of them about us and our life here at Perfection City, if it comes to that."

"True, I daresay there are," said Madame. "One should be charitable."

Olive was evidently ill at ease, and Madame drawing from a totally different experience of life her own conclusions, became convinced that Ezra's wife was carrying on a secret acquaintanceship with a man of whom he thought very ill.

Madame's position as leader at Perfection City gave her many rights and imposed certain duties. She considered that of private admonition as one of them. She did not speak for some moments, and the two walked along in silence. Madame was debating in her own mind whether she should speak to Olive and endeavour to turn her from the dangerous path towards which she seemed to be directing her steps; or whether she should keep silence and let her destiny be accomplished. She reflected that if she spoke to Olive, that rather high-spirited young woman would probably resent her interference, and might possibly complain to Ezra, with the result of estranging him from herself. On the other hand, if she left the silly wife to go her foolish way, she would break her husband's heart. Madame's well-shaped lips curled with a smile of contempt for herself as these thoughts passed rapidly through her brain. What a fool she was to stir in the matter! Let the giddy girl follow her own impulses and then—No, no! She would be true to her best self, she would put forth a hand and draw back the blind fool from the precipice that lay before her.

She spoke therefore to Olive in that soft quiet voice of hers that seemed to have more power of arresting the attention and holding it than the roar of an avalanche.

"I think you are, perhaps, not acquainted with Mr. Cotterell's character," said she. "I am sure you would not wish to associate with a bad man."

"Why do you think he is a bad man? Do you know him?"

"No, I don't know him, but I am sure I am right in saying that he is a man of loose morals," said Madame.

"I don't believe it," said Olive.

"Why not? How can you know?"

"Because I have talked with him a great deal, and he speaks like a man with high aspirations, and not at all like the bad man you say he is."

"But what can you know of a man's real character from a chance word or two as you run across him in an afternoon's stroll?" observed Madame.

"I don't judge from a chance word, I have had long talks with him."

"Indeed! and where? Do you meet him here at the spring then, so often?"

"I never met him at the spring before, but I used to meet him pretty often, when I was out cattle-hunting and he would generally accompany me for a bit. Sometimes too, he used to pass our house on his way cattle-hunting, and then he would look in and water his horse and stop to talk to me for a time," said Olive in explanation.

"Really!" said Madame looking keenly at her companion, "and did Ezra know of these visits?"

"Ezra said he wasn't to come any more, and I told Mr. Cotterell so to-day."

"Oh! and what did he say?"

"He called Ezra a dog in the manger, and I do think Ezra oughtn't to be so harsh about Mr. Cotterell. He would like to be a better man, I know, if he had any chance, and people were kind to him."

"Did he intimate that you could influence him towards the better way?"

"I don't see why I can't try to use my influence in trying to make my fellow-creatures happier and better. You and Ezra are always talking about doing good that way. Why do you want to stop me the moment I see a chance of doing a little good?"

"Because you would only do harm."

"No, I shouldn't. A woman has great influence over a man. He said so himself."

"Mr. Cotterell said so?" inquired Madame.

"Yes."

"It is a very dangerous thing for a young woman to attempt to influence men of that sort."

"You don't know what sort he is, nor anything about him. You are only following reports. And how can you talk about the danger of influencing men? That is just what you are always doing yourself."

"With me it is quite different," said Madame hastily.

"That is what everybody says to me whenever I want to do what other people find it right to do. I hate being treated like a baby."

"You are very young and very pretty, child, and that makes it all the more necessary for your friends to guard you against dangers which you don't perceive as clearly as they do."

"I hate being young and—well—pretty, if it's always going to make me be treated like that," said Olive angrily.

"Like what?"

"Like a naughty child. That's what Ezra does, and he goes to you to ask what he should do to me, you know he does." She was beginning to cry, just like a naughty child.

Madame smiled contemptuously as she glanced at her companion. "What could have possessed that quiet reserved Ezra to marry such a feather-headed vain little puss?" she thought bitterly.

Olive dried her eyes angrily, she saw the contempt expressed by Madame's curling lips, and her pride was thoroughly aroused.

"I want to know why things are different as soon as they apply to me?" she asked with doubtful grammar but unmistakable import. "It isn't this once only, but it is always so. Personal liberty is the corner-stone of Perfection City, that is what you are here for, to enjoy liberty and protest against things. Mary Winkle won't take her husband's name, and dresses like a fright, and nobody minds. She's free. But as soon as I try a little flight of my own, that doesn't hurt anybody, I'm to be popped into a cage, and you and Ezra come and shut the door on me. I met this man by chance and liked talking to him. He is well-mannered and well educated, and likes the same books as I do, and has travelled and could tell me heaps and heaps of interesting things. He wasn't forever talking in the same little muddling circle, and wasn't always full of himself. He tried to interest me. You are an educated woman, Madame, and you know as well as I do that, except for you and Ezra, there is not an educated person in Perfection City, nor one who has the same tastes as I have. Mr. Cotterell used to come and talk to me, and I liked it; then Ezra gets very angry, says he is a bad man, and forbids my seeing him. He forbids me, mind you. Not a bit the sort of language you would expect in Perfection City, but I believe in wifely obedience and I obeyed him. I told Mr. Cotterell he must not come to see me any more, and he won't do so. He always showed the best spirit in everything he said, and I won't believe he is so very wicked just on mere report. We once had a horse-thief and murderer to stay to supper, and we did not inquire into his character before we asked him to stop and rest and feed his horse. Mr. Cotterell said my influence might help him to be a better man, and perhaps it might. At all events, I want to know why I wasn't to try to influence him, and I want to know why Perfection City ideas, when they make for freedom, are not applicable to me, but have to be all turned upside down when I come into play? Can you, Madame, answer me that?"

Madame was considerably dumbfounded by this attack delivered so unexpectedly and so very straight from the shoulder. She hastily recast her idea that Olive was a silly little fool, and most unaccountably found herself anxiously seeking about for means of defence.

"The fact of the matter is, you are too pretty to do these things," she replied, helplessly telling the truth in her extremity.

"Can Perfection City then only succeed if all the women are ugly?" asked Olive scornfully. "You had better not proclaim that fact, or you'll have all the women running away."

Madame was in the habit of being worshipped by men, and was not at all prepared to have her remarks ridiculed by a slip of a girl. She did not like it, and therefore replied with some asperity,

"You are really too silly, Sister Olive. You must surely perceive that there is great danger in your associating with Mr. Cotterell on so familiar a footing, that, in short, he may fall in love with you, and I presume you can understand the danger of that."

"Precisely, a fresh set of laws must, as usual, be applied to me, and not those which govern the rest of you," said Olive calmly.

"I don't understand to what you refer," said Madame looking at her doubtfully.

"Mr. Cotterell knew from the outset that I was a married woman. I don't see the alarmingness of the danger that he might fall in love with me, simply because we talked together. The idea has only struck you in reference to me; it does not seem to have done so with regard to the similar circumstances of you and Ezra."

Madame turned white with anger. "How dare you insult me by such an insinuation?" she exclaimed.

"I didn't dare until after you had first given utterance to the insinuation against me," replied Olive, with provoking calmness.

Madame turned as if she could have struck her, but she controlled herself with a desperate effort.

"It seems to me, Sister Olive, that your remarks are very ill-judged," she said in a voice that shook in spite of her. "I have no wish to bandy words with you. I spoke merely out of a desire to do my duty, and to save you, if possible, from a danger which I imagined I foresaw more clearly than you did. I see that your words were prompted by quite another wish than to seek advice or counsel in a difficult moment."

"I sought for neither advice or counsel," returned Olive. "I simply wanted to discover, if possible, how to fit the theories of Perfection City, which I know pretty well by heart now, into the practice as applied to me."

Madame looked at her with eyes of anger and even of hate, and Olive, conscious of having been almost more successful than she had imagined possible in argument with so distinguished a mind, returned the look with one suggestive of triumph. Alas for the perfect harmony of Perfection City!

"I am surprised, I will not say pained, because you would care little for that, but I am surprised, I repeat, at such words in the mouth of Ezra Weston's wife. He must have been strangely mistaken in your character, or you cannot have revealed your true self to him, for I cannot imagine him binding himself for life to a mate who scorns and flouts in this manner what he holds so dear. You are mocking the principles to which he has devoted his life. You are too foolish to see what you are doing, but one day you will be punished, and then perhaps you will repent—when it will be too late."

Madame turned and walked rapidly away, leaving Olive feeling very angry and very much frightened as well.

That evening Napoleon Pompey carried a note

and a small parcel to Madame, who guessed pretty well what it was. The note was brief, it contained but these words:

"I thought you sent the bracelet as a present, therefore I accepted it and was grateful: now I know you sent it as a reproof, therefore I return it."

## CHAPTER XII.

### THE PRAIRIE FIRE.

THE summer had been a particularly dry one, and since the beginning of July not a drop of rain had fallen. The water-melons revelled in the heat, and Olive revelled in the water-melons: for by a blessed compensation of Nature the hotter and drier the land, the cooler and juicier the water-melons seem to be. The water-melon of the western prairie is as different from the pallid green-fleshed vegetable which masquerades under its name in this country, as the full moon of the heavens is superior to the lime-light article manufactured for use on the stage. The real prairie water-melon is an enormous affair, being about as large as the roll of rugs without which fussy gentlemen consider it impossible to travel. The skin is of the darkest green and as hard as a board, a most unripe-looking object at all times. Indeed the only way one can find out the condition of a water-melon's insides is by surgical operation. You simply cut out a plug about an inch square from the top side of the melon, and look to see if the flesh has turned crimson at the centre. If it is still white or pale pink you know the psychological moment, when the truly wise will eat the melon, has not yet arrived. Accordingly you put back the plug, and leave the sun to work a little longer on it, at a temperature of a hundred and twenty or so. Since it never rains at the melon season of the year, the plug does not do any harm if left on the top side, but the beginner sometimes leaves it on the lower side, with the result that all the water runs away. It is a curious fact, but the water of a melon, even of one picked in the middle of a scorching hot day, never seems tepid. It is always cool and refreshing, even at times when ordinary water tastes unutterably mawkish owing to the excessive heat. The crimson spongy flesh, specked with purple-black seeds, is eaten in moderation or in immoderation according to the taste of the individual, but the water is always greedily drunk up by everybody. The scorching winds of the plains seem to dry one's very marrow, and nothing can exceed the thirst of a man who is obliged to be out all day in such weather and to work hard at the same time. Animals, too, suffer from extreme thirst, and after a morning's ploughing when the farm horses are brought up to water, they drink and drink and drink, swelling visibly under one's eye, as if they were india-rubber horses under the action of some new patent inflator. They are never stinted in their drink and swallow bucketsful before attacking their corn.

But to return to our water-melons.

Napoleon Pompey used to bring up a wheelbarrow full from the melon patch each morning for the day's consumption. He, like a true negro, was inordinately fond of melons, or "millions" as he called them, and would have sucked them all day long if left to his own devices. Whenever he had to go anywhere in the waggon, as occasionally happened, he would lay in a store of "millions," and lay himself beside them, and suck them, just as if he were a black caterpillar of unlimited capacity. The horses meantime, far too oppressed with the heat to require much attention, would plod along with their eyes shut, trying to keep out the glaring light. There was nothing to stumble over or fall into, so the driving became of the most elementary pattern, requiring only an occasional rattle of the reins and a comment or two, such as: "Yo', Reb, g' 'long will yer, g' out o' dat."

Olive during this period found the heat stifling, and used to sit out of doors on the shady side of the house, until the terrible wind blew up from the Plains, when she would flee as before the breath of a volcano, and shutting herself tight up in her room with closed doors and windows, would gasp through the visitation as best she might. She was no worse off than anyone else, and the nights were always cool and refreshing. That was an unspeakable blessing. All this heat dried up the thick prairie grass until it was like a vast plain of dry hay standing erect.

The corn crop at Perfection City had turned out

exceptionally good. There was ample for all the needs of the Community and a good surplus which was to be sold at Mapleton in order to enable them to buy some farm-machinery that was greatly needed. Consequently the whole Community worked hard at getting in the corn so as to be early in the market. The heavy ears of corn with their twenty rows of golden yellow grains were stripped off the tall stalks by hand: a most limb-lacerating job, for the "shucks," or coverings to the ear, are masses of fibrous leaves with saw-like edges. These edges have the power of cutting an exposed finger in a most painful manner, and they are by no means loath to use the power.

All this hurry and concentration of the workers upon the corn-field was possible only if every other sort of work was neglected for the moment. It seemed the wisest plan to hasten off with their harvest in spite of the risk, and, unused as they were to prairie life, yet even they realized that there was some risk in thus leaving their farms unprotected. Ezra was perfectly aware of it, but like so many people he shut his eyes and hoped for good luck. He spoke to Olive on the subject.

"If anyone so much as drops a lighted match on the prairie we shall be lost," he said.

"Why, what do you mean?" asked his wife in surprise. She was still so new to the prairie that she did not understand to what he referred. They happened to be on that outside landing of the stairs which looked out over the wide boundless western prairie. This stairway from its position made an exceptionally good place from which to take a survey of the whole prospect.

"That grass is like tinder, and if anybody leaves a coal of fire burning at his camping-place or drops his pipe, the thing will catch in a second, and if there is a strong west wind we shall see about as bad a prairie fire as we care to."

"Oh, but that's dreadful! What shall we do?" said Olive, much alarmed.

"As soon as our corn is sold at Mapleton, we shall plough all round Perfection City and back-fire, if we can only get a calm day. We must not back-fire in a high wind, because that would probably start a prairie fire and just cause the very mischief we want to guard against. It would take fifty people to keep a line of fire under control for a mile's length with grass like that and a strong wind." So spoke Ezra, critically scanning the horizon for any sign of smoke which might betoken danger. He was very uneasy, and the fierce west wind, which seemed never weary of blowing, made him all the more anxious, as it might prevent them guarding themselves by running the usual belt of burnt prairie all around Perfection City.

It was not a light job to get a safety belt of about four miles long, for that was the circumference of the portion of their land fenced in, and it was an impossible one in the face of a high wind with their small force—unless indeed they did as selfish individualists did, namely let the fire go and burn out whom it liked and what it liked once they were themselves safe. The Pioneers refused to be guilty of this act of treachery to the common weal of the inhabitants of the prairie. It is a comparatively easy thing to keep one line of fire safe and so protect your own fields; the real difficulty begins when you want to stop the fire from spreading in other directions as well. Most of the settlers back-fired their own land, and left Providence or the Devil to see to the result as regards their neighbours. The Pioneers had naturally a higher standard of public duty than this, therefore they did not back-fire in the high wind.

The corn being stripped off the stalks, Olive's fairy forest was sadly mutilated, for the great ears were all gone and many of the streaming leaves were torn away; the walk to the spring, therefore, was no longer so delightful as it had been earlier in the summer. Still she and Diana used to go there pretty often, especially since Napoleon Pompey was always kept busy helping in the field. Coming up from the spring one afternoon just before sundown, she was amazed to see her husband galloping madly along the far side of the field on Queen Katherine, the big brown mare, her harness banging her hot flanks at every stride, while Napoleon Pompey on Rebel was tearing after him waving his tattered old straw hat. Olive for a moment or two stared in blank amazement at them, and then began to run towards the house which appeared to be their destination also. Ezra and Napoleon Pompey with frantic gestures seemed to invite her attention to the setting sun, now sinking to rest like a shimmering copper ball. She looked, but saw nothing except the molten mass, unless it were a faint blue haze on the horizon, the result, as she supposed, of the intense heat.

When Olive reached the house a few moments later, it was to see her husband going hurriedly down the road to the bars on the other side of the house. The horses were hitched to the plough and were trotting fast, while Napoleon Pompey was urging them on with voice and whip. The plough, unaccustomed to such speed, was jerking from side to side. A moment's halt at the bars, while Napoleon Pompey threw down the rails, and Ezra turning round put both hands to his mouth and shouted " Fire " in a long re-echoing whoop. He wheeled around then and seizing his plough-handles set off at a hand-gallop, bounding along with his ungainly implement.

Now Olive understood what that blue haze meant. It was a prairie fire coming down on them from the west along with a fierce wind. Oh dear! oh dear! What should she do? There must be something women could help at, in such a moment, if she only knew what. But who to ask? Everybody was far away, and the dreadful fire began to show up now that the sun was no longer casting such bright rays.

"Come 'long, git yer shingle," shouted a familiar voice behind her.

"Oh, Willette, is that you? What shall I do? It's a fire, and I don't know what's wanted."

"Nothin' but a shingle an' a box o' matches. Quick now! We'll hev ter pike, you bet. Pa and Ma is out firin' a'ready down yonder, 'side our house."

"I am so glad you've come," said Olive hurrying along with two wooden shingles under her arm.

The shingles were merely the thin wooden "slates" with which the houses were roofed. When thoroughly dried they are admirably adapted for spreading a fire from house to house in a street, and accordingly they are now prohibited by law in most towns and cities. On the prairie they were used in emergencies as paddles to keep the back-firing within limits.

"Yes, Ma said she 'lowed you wouldn't know the fust thing ter do," remarked Willette complacently. "An' Pa said he reckoned school larnin' in the East could make folks more like nateral born fools than anything under the sun."

Olive was very little obliged to the Wright and Winkle spouses for their opinion of her. She remained therefore silent.

They soon reached the furrows that were being so desperately ploughed by Ezra and his foam-covered horses. The swift twilight was almost upon them, but they could see Wright urging his horses along the south side of the land nearest his house, while

## THE PRAIRIE FIRE. 149

away across at the east side of Perfection City Brother Dummy was thundering along with his waggon bringing up his plough to the rescue, and that completed all the horse-power of the Community. Little tongues of flame here and there along the furrows denoted that the back-firing had begun in several spots. Meanwhile the sky was reddening up with the reflection of the on-coming conflagration, and the fierce wind blew ever harder directly from its long blood-red line.

"Now you jes' set afire 'long hyar, front this hyar furrow," said Willette, kneeling down with her matches and starting the fire as she spoke. "Now then, yo' jes' see to that, an' don't yo' let that ar fire hop over behind yer, or it'll be worse nor nothin'."

"What am I to do?" asked Olive trembling with excitement and fear, it was all so strange and alarming. "I never saw a fire and don't know anything about it," she added.

"Jes' paddle it out with yer shingle, ef it gits over. There ain't no sight o' larnin' wanted for that," said Willette in scorn. "Mind yer ends, and look after tongues in the middle. They'll be powerful handy at jumpin' over this hyar furrow, and you mustn't let the fire git away from yer, else yo'll be clear done for. Keep yer eyes behind yer and min' the back line," said Willette walking away.

"Land o' liberty! look at that!"

Willette made one bound behind Olive and commenced furiously beating the ground with her wooden paddle, while Olive, bewildered, turned round to see that she had indeed let the fire get behind her even as Willette was uttering her warning.

"We 'uns would ha' been clear burnt out in one grasshopper's jump on'y I was there," said Willette looking critically to see if any little spark of fire lingered in the tall grass which could by any chance start into life again.

"Oh I can never manage it! What shall I do?"

"Be spry and—Look at that again now!" Willette sprang to a new place and beat the ground. She was back again in an instant, here there and every where, with the activity of a monkey, beating down for dear life, whenever the fire crossed the narrow base-line of the up-turned sod, and as the wind was high it was frequently doing this. Constant vigilance was required, especially as Ezra had only had time to run a few furrows with the plough, instead of a band five or six feet wide.

"Powerful heavy work in this hyar high wind," said the child, "and on'y that ar furrow to start from."

Willette was in her element. Not an inch of the line escaped her lynx-eye, and all the while she kept giving advice to Olive, who stood in awe of her superior practical knowledge in this emergency.

"Now this hyar fire's agoin' to spread along, an' yo' jes' got ter mind this end by yerself."

She darted twenty yards away and paddled out a flame and came back, her face begrimed with smoke and dirt, so that she looked not unlike the nigger whose modes of speech she so much affected.

"You jes' take off that ar hat and them big skirts, else you'll be burnt to death right hyar," said Willette surveying Olive with considerable disapproval.

Willette's hickory trousers and shirt were exactly the thing for a prairie fire in a high wind, as indeed they were for most of the occupations that fell to her lot. What with the constant bounding backwards and forwards over the flame, Olive indeed thought that she had better accept the advice and slip off her wide calico skirt which was forever in the way and might easily catch fire. She put it along with her hat just at the top of the slope where Weddell's Gully began, where she could easily get them next day, if all went well.

It was night now and would have been quite dark but for the bright glare from the fire. All the inhabitants of the Community were out working desperately. Olive paddled down her fire and kept her line bravely for a couple of hours, in spite of choking smoke and clouds of dust and many a burn. Willette was far away, lost in the darkness, following her end of the fire, and only became visible as she leaped backwards and forwards over her line of fire like some agile fiend engaged in roasting its victims. Olive was all alone. She felt very much frightened, for she did not know what might happen, nor what in any new emergency she would have to do. She wished somebody would come, for it was a strange experience to be in the black night and lurid glare all alone minding a fire. The air was full of the burnt fluff from the big fire, and the roar as it now had come near was terrifying. True the worst of it was passing to the south, and their land was now pretty well guarded on all sides. Suddenly the cheerful black face of Napoleon Pompey appeared in the light of the flame.

"Oh, Pompey, I'm so glad you've come. Where is everybody?" said Olive, overjoyed to see a human being once more.

"Wal, Mis' Ollie, I on'y jes' take ole plough to de bars. We'uns rip up dat furrow golly spry. Done turn de hosses loose."

"Why, the poor horses will be burnt!" exclaimed Olive in dismay.

"Dem hosses, dey dre'ful cute critters. Dey go off slap to de bottom lan'. You bet hosses knows mos' as well nor white folks 'bout prairie fires. I come min' yo' fire fo' yer, Mis' Ollie. Ole man he done tole me."

"Very well, you can take my shingle then. There is not much more, I suppose, to be done now, only you must keep both edges between the two furrows here. They told me not to let it get away and run down into the Gully. Do you understand?"

"You bet," replied Napoleon Pompey who knew far better than Olive could tell him just what should be done.

"I am going to get my hat and skirt. I left them near the corner of Weddell's Gully. I think I will just run across the old field and get them: it will be much shorter than going all the way round by the furrows. It will be light enough to see yet awhile so I can follow the path through the Gully."

Olive looked at the fire that was fast roaring its way towards the south-east, and deciding it would easily light her on her way she tripped off and disappeared in the gloom down towards the Gully.

In a few minutes Napoleon Pompey began to show signs of immense excitement.

"Golly Ned! I never seed yonder. Mis' Ollie whar yo' be? Come back! Come back, Mis' Ollie! Golly! Golly!"

He ran violently backwards and forwards along his line of fire, which, however, he dared not leave, exclaiming "Golly!" and "Oh Lordy!" at every step. In a minute or two he ran into Ezra who was coming along to fetch Olive home, if she was still there.

"Lordy! dat yo', Mas'r Ezra. Yo' go right 'long down dish hyar Gully. Mis' Ollie she down dar."

Ezra was dead beat. He could scarcely drag his limbs along. The terrific exertion of that furious ploughing, coming at the end of a long and hard day's work, had almost over-taxed even his iron frame.

"I thought I would find her here on my way home," he said languidly. "We are pretty safe now.

Tell her to come back with the others. I'm going home to get something to eat."

"No, sir-ee," said Napoleon Pompey vehemently. "You' hain't gwine ter do dat. Golly Ned! Yo' dunno see. Mis' Ollie she done gone down inter de Gully, fetch ole hat. Dat fire. Yo' see dat fire startin' up yonder, she never seed dat, I didn't see it nudder nohow: dat fire'll crope up an' cotch her."

"My God! where is she?" cried Ezra, roused to sudden energy as it dawned upon him what Napoleon Pompey was explaining.

"Down de Gully dar, she say she gwine down dar."

"Amongst those tall weeds and that fire coming on! Oh my God!"

His fatigue was all gone now. He leaped forward and sprang with desperate bounds down the straggling path towards Weddell's Gully, where, in a deserted field once tilled by that individual, prairie weeds were growing to the height of six feet and more, they had dry stalks and fluffy downy heads that would burn like petroleum, if the fire once touch them. It was down there that Olive had gone, all ignorant of that tiny red line creeping slowly around the brow of the hill, up against the wind, and now approaching that very spot with vicious little tongues of red flame. No wonder Ezra bounded along the pathway, no wonder his heart beat ready to burst, and no wonder if his voice sounded harsh and choking as he cried

"Olive! Olive! Olive!" again and again until his brain reeled. He got no answer except the crackle of the fire. He stumbled along not knowing which way to turn, and twice fell forward as his foot caught in the tangled grass. He staggered to his feet and raising his agonised face cried in a harsh whisper, "Oh God! my wife, my wife!" He tried to shout again, but his dry throat made no articulate sound. His temples seemed bursting, he dashed forward blindly, not knowing where to look for Olive in the horrid darkness, soon to be turned into still more horrid light. His foot struck against an old rail at the edge of Weddell's deserted field, he fell heavily, hitting his head against the projecting end of the rail, rolled over and lay still. The little flames crept nearer and nearer lapping out their malicious red tongues as if in anticipation.

## CHAPTER XIII.

#### THE RESCUE.

MADAME had worked hard with the rest in beating back the fire, and now that she saw that their united efforts had been successful and that Perfection City was safe, she, in company with Balthasar, was going the circuit of the defences of their home, just to see that there remained nothing further for her to do. In the course of time she came to Napoleon Pompey, who was in charge of the last scrap of back-firing, intent on maintaining guard and on effecting a complete junction of the two lines of fire, so as not to leave so much as a handsbreadth of standing grass whereby the enemy might even at the last minute burst in upon them. This finishing of the circle was important, and the lad was in the midst of his work and his distress when Madame loomed out through the darkness.

"Oh, Lordy, dey is both burned, dey is! Oh Lordy! Oh Lordy," cried Napoleon Pompey the instant he set eyes upon Madame.

"Who is burned?" asked Madame in bewilderment, well used to the extravagant modes of speech indulged in by negroes.

"Mis' Ollie an' Mas'r Ezra fo' shu'."

"Are you mad, fool, what do you mean?" said Madame furiously.

"Mis' Ollie done gone in der Gully ter fetch ole hat, an' de fire's crope up, an' it'll cotch her, oh Lordy! oh Lordy! An' Mas'r Ezra he done gone ter fin' her down dar," said the boy, beginning to whimper.

Madame gripped his shoulder with a grasp of iron.

"Be quiet, and tell me what you mean. Sister Olive has gone home, I passed her myself with her hat under her arm, and she told me to tell Ezra she had gone back."

"De Lord be praised!" ejaculated Napoleon Pompey. "Den it's on'y Mas'r Ezra'll be burnt. Yah, you lemme go!"

This exclamation was in answer to the sudden pressure of Madame's hand, which was like the clutch of a vice.

"Where is Ezra? Tell me or I'll wring your neck," she said in a voice the like of which Napoleon Pompey had never heard before in his life.

"Down dar," said he terrified, pointing to the Gully.

"Show me where he started from."

Madame still kept her hand upon Napoleon Pompey who hurried to the spot where Ezra had stood.

"Dar's his shingle, what he done drap when he run."

"Ha!" said Madame pouncing upon the shingle. "Here, Balthasar, here sweetheart!"

The dog came up to her, and she passed her trembling hands over his long ears and whispered to him half crying, half coaxing. "Here, dear heart, do this for me or I die."

She put the shingle to his nose. He sniffed, raised his long and pointed head. Then she lay upon the ground coaxing him to put his nose down. He sniffed again, took a step to the right, to the left, back, then forward. Madame followed clasping the shingle to her bosom and murmuring cooing words of love to her dog. He raised his great tan head and gave a long deep bay that echoed far and wide.

"Golly! She gwine ter run him down like he nigger slave," said Napoleon Pompey with a shiver, as he heard the dog's voice.

Balthasar set off and Madame kept close at his heels. It was easy enough, for the trail was fresh and strong. In three minutes they stood beside the motionless form of Ezra at the brink of the tall weeds, and Balthasar whined in anxiety as Madame lifted his head and called upon him in agonised tones. Just then the sky was lit up with a lurid glare. The first red tongue had tasted the dry fluffy weeds on Weddell's abandoned farm. Madame, startled by the flame, sprang to her feet and gave one hasty glance around.

Ezra lay motionless. She stepped a few paces into the shorter grass of the ordinary prairie and set it on fire. The little ring of flame spread on all sides, like the ripple from a stone cast into still water. Then she paddled out the fire on the side next Ezra, and the ripple of fire continued to spread rapidly in a sort of broken circle. The roar of the burning weeds was like the on-coming of an avalanche. Madame turned to Ezra and seizing him under the shoulders dragged him backwards within the safety of her oasis of burnt prairie. He was a big man and a heavy one, but her arm seemed endowed with more than mortal strength. She dragged him further and further within the circle, and then seeing that he was out of all danger, she sat down beside him and took his head in her lap. She opened his collar and fanned him with her hat. The now brightly burning weeds made it light as day, and she could see that he looked pale even under the blackened smoke that smeared his face, but his pulse was beating, he was only hurt and stunned, not dead.

Balthasar was terrified. Ringed round by fire and with the ground where he stood still smoking hot, what dog would not be alarmed? He lifted up his voice once more in a long howl, and then sniffing at Ezra gave a sweeping lick with his tongue all over his face.

"Ah! Ollie! Where are you? Come!" said Ezra, roused by this combined demonstration. He raised his head in a weak and bewildered way. Madame placed her hand on his forehead as he sank down again. He put his own hand up and taking hers said: "Little wife!"

Madame shivered, and then steadying her voice said, "Olive is quite safe!"

Ezra started up.

"Why, what are you doing here? Where is my wife?"

"I came to tell you that Olive had gone home, and that she had got her hat all right. She never was in any danger at all. It was a mistake on the part of that negro boy."

"Madame!" began Ezra.

"Dear friend," said she.

"I feel so strange and bewildered, I don't seem to know what has happened."

"Lay your head down again," said Madame, very gently. "You have had a blow. You will soon be all right."

Ezra's head sank again into her lap. He gave a deep sigh.

"You came down here into the Gully after Olive who, according to the negro, had gone in search of her hat. You could not surely have realized that the fire was coming up against the wind and that it would be death to be caught among the weeds."

"I knew, I knew," said Ezra. "That was why I came. Olive was here."

"But she wasn't, she never had been here at all," interrupted Madame.

"I shouted, but no answer came. I could not find Olive. I remember the awful agony of it. My head seemed turning to fire and I couldn't find Olive. I don't remember any more."

"You fell and knocked yourself senseless," said Madame.

"Is Olive safe? Tell me, are you sure Olive is safe?"

"Didn't I tell you I passed her on her way home?" said Madame a little sharply.

"But this fire!" exclaimed Ezra, starting up. "We must get out of this."

"Hush, lie down again," said Madame, her voice dropping again into its tone of caressing entreaty. "Your head must be still giddy or you would perceive that we are surrounded. We can't get out until the fires meet and extinguish each other. Rest and be patient."

Ezra saw that this was true. They were entirely surrounded by a ring of retreating fire, the heat from which was oppressive. He sat down again, but did not lay his head in Madame's lap. Perhaps it was because he felt less giddy.

He asked her how she came there, and Madame very briefly told him, dwelling not at all upon her share in finding him, but rather upon the sagacity of Balthasar. Ezra, however, was not to be deceived.

"You risked your life for me this night, Madame," he said slowly, when she had finished speaking.

"Possibly. I never thought about it. I could not leave you here to die, to be burnt to death. Had the case been reversed you would have come to my rescue."

"You are the most generous of mortals, the noblest of women," said Ezra earnestly. "It was assuredly the brightest day of my life that led me across your path. You taught me how to live, and to-night your generous hand has saved me from death."

"Hush!" said Madame faintly.

"I owe my life to you," repeated Ezra. "What shall I do to repay such a debt?"

"Am I a usurer that I should exact my pound of flesh?" answered Madame.

"Usurer!" exclaimed Ezra. "That is indeed the last word to be applied to you. Is a usurer one who is always giving? Giving from her wealth freely and without stint? Is a usurer one who is ever helping and directing into the paths of righteousness those who are feeble and faltering of step? Ah, Madame, I never can half tell you all that I owe you! How narrow and selfish would my life have been but for you! Devoted to petty cares, absorbed in personal ambitions, rejoicing in sordid gains,—such would have been my fate, only Providence brought me to you to be taught, guided, elevated, purified. My life is yours, you have made it, dearest, wisest, best, of friends."

"And Olive?" said Madame quietly.

"Ah, there too shall be your handiwork seen," said Ezra. "My little Olive is very young. Sometimes I think her mind is even younger than her body, and she is barely twenty, you know, a mere child and easily moulded."

Madame remembering her last encounter with Olive, seemed to recall very little that was either childlike or plastic in the concluding portion of their conversation, but she did not say so to Ezra who went on talking.

"She often, however, puzzles me, she has such sudden freaks and fancies, as if her heart was a wild creature not fully tamed and ever dashing against the bars of its environment. I sometimes feel that I have not the necessary wisdom or tact to guide and counsel her. She seems to need someone who is wiser and more skilful than I am. Sometimes I fear she does not quite realise the responsibilities of life. The problems which have come up before us and which cry aloud for solution, seem to her but trivial matters that may be trusted to settle themselves. We must endeavour, dear friend, to arouse Olive's enthusiasm about Perfection City. She is capable of the highest and noblest aspirations, but her heart must be turned into the right direction. She evinces a certain hesitancy in throwing herself into our work and aims."

"Perhaps she is opposed to the whole thing," suggested Madame.

"That cannot be," replied Ezra earnestly. "She must see as we do, when she comes thoroughly to understand our motives in founding Perfection City. I look to you, Madame, to open her eyes to the truth."

"Ah!" said Madame laconically, and then she added, after a moment's pause, "I will ask you to do one thing for me."

"Anything you ask I will do if it is in my power," said Ezra.

"Do not tell Olive of your fall here, nor of the danger you were in, nor of my coming to find you."

After a moment of puzzled silence Ezra said, "Of course your wishes are to me law. But may I ask why you make such a request?"

"Perhaps I am judging wrongly, but I am acting as if Olive had the same feelings as I should have. If I were in her place, I should hate it."

"Why?" asked Ezra in surprise.

Madame rose up, her pale face illumined by the light of the fire.

"If I loved a man," she said, beginning very quietly, but her voice gathered in intensity as she spoke. "If I loved a man, I could not bear it. To think that my love had failed him in his sorest need. He was lying stunned, helpless, within the clutch of deadly peril, and I went home unwarned, leaving him to his fate, all unconscious of the whole thing, while another woman—not I, but another woman— went to his rescue, another woman—not I—found him, saved him, drew him out of danger, while I walked heedlessly home. I should hate myself, I should hate—ah! I should hate to the verge of killing that other woman who had saved him. That is the way I should feel, if I loved."

She concluded hastily, her voice dropping to a whisper. Ezra looked up at her in amazement.

"Yours is a many-sided nature. I never suspected you could feel like that. I never thought of you as being—as capable of——" he stopped in confusion.

"Ah yes! You never thought of me as being able to love—to love a man and not an impersonal cause. Ah yes! You never quite looked upon me as a mere woman."

"I have always regarded you as something higher than a mere woman," said Ezra.

"Listen," she said, sitting down again beside him. "You have yet to know me—the woman, I mean, and not the pioneer of Perfection City. My father was a man of passionate nature. He had fine instincts, but these were not developed. He was a Russian noble. I come of very good blood, as they say in the old world."

"I always knew you were of distinguished birth," said Ezra.

"Not at all, quite the contrary," said Madame, with a laugh that sounded harsh. "My father was a wild, self-willed Russian noble. He was to have married a lady of princely house, only that he refused to do one thing which they made a condition of the marriage."

"What was that?"

"To give up my mother. Do you understand? He could not marry the princess, and he sacrificed wealth, position, and worldly honour, because he would not give up the pale-haired English girl whom he loved passionately, and who was my mother. She died, and my father died too, not many years afterwards. He did what he could for me by leaving me his fortune and the permission to bear his name, to which I had no legal right. From my mother I inherited my brain, but my heart I inherited from my father. Now let us go."

"Must we?" said Ezra, to whom Madame's sudden confession had been full of interest. "There is nothing further for us to do. Perfection City is safe."

"But we must return to real life, Brother Ezra. Sitting here, ringed around with fire, we were alone in a world of our own. For a few moments we lived for each other, as it were. Our spirits communed, and I opened my heart to you as never before to mortal being. Now we must go back to real life again. See the fires are all out, and the world is itself again—all dark."

Ezra rose to his feet and staggered a little, as Madame perceived from the stumble he made. She seemed preternaturally acute, and to be able to understand by the help of some new sense, for she put out her hand

and touched his arm, "Lean on me, brother, you are still giddy from your accident. We will walk very slowly."

Ezra, feeling indeed faint enough, gratefully accepted the proffered help and put his hand within her arm; thus very slowly they started back towards the house through the inky black night. "Friend, what I said is to be locked in your breast, a secret," said Madame.

"I fully understand that," replied Ezra, "and I feel it a high honour that you should have chosen me as the repository of the secret of your life. It is safe, nay more, it is sacred, with me."

It took them a long time in the intense darkness to reach Ezra's house where a light was glimmering from the window. When they at length reached the bars, Madame said, "I will not go in. Oh, I know what you would say, but I would prefer not. Olive would resent my bringing you back to her."

"You mistake Olive utterly," said Ezra earnestly. "Believe me, hers is a simple nature, she would have no such feelings as you think."

"Perhaps you are right, and that she is a child in mind and not yet a woman in heart. Possibly I endow her with feelings she could not even understand. I judge her by myself, and maybe all the while her little soul is possessed with nothing but content at the thought that her pretty hat is all safe. The butterfly must not be blamed if it does not rise as high as the lark. Farewell."

Olive was waiting for him impatiently, anxiously.

"Oh Ezra, where have you been? And isn't your face black? You are every whit as black as Napoleon Pompey. Wasn't it fun?"

"Fun? What was fun?" asked Ezra languidly.

"Why, the fire of course, now that it is all over. It was so exciting. I was as hungry as a hawk when I came in. I really could not wait, so I had supper. You must have yours this very minute. Do you know, it is one o'clock at night, and you have not tasted a morsel of food since twelve o'clock yesterday? Do you realize that?"

She bustled around and got his supper ready, chatting brightly all the while over the incidents of the fire, making fun and merriment out of them all. Ezra sat stupidly watching her, his head throbbing so heavily that he could scarcely think. He could eat nothing when the supper was ready, and Olive felt aggrieved. "I think you might, just to please me. It would do you good, for you must be hungry, I should think."

He swallowed a few morsels and said he would go to bed, that rest was what he most needed, his head ached badly. He was thankful she made no inquiries after his adventures during that eventful night. He would have found it difficult to tell a connected tale with that pain in his head. He asked Olive if she had gone down into the Gully.

"No," she said, "I started to go, but it was darker than I thought, so I came up again and followed round by the high prairie where there was a chance of meeting somebody. I came home with Willette."

"The fire did get into the old field after all," said Ezra.

"And were the weeds burnt?"

"Yes."

"Oh! I wish I had been there to see. Wasn't it a lovely blaze-up?"

"Yes, it blazed up," said Ezra.

Olive didn't notice that he seemed ill, he thought with some bitterness. Madame would have divined it, no matter how hard he had tried to conceal the fact. After all, it was not her fault that she was made differently. The butterfly was not to be blamed if it did not soar as high as the lark.

## CHAPTER XIV.

### COTTERELL "WANTED."

The day after the fire was an idle one at Perfection City. No one felt able to work, Ezra least of all. He lay upon the floor of the kitchen with a wet handkerchief on his head, and several times he asked Olive not to make so much noise. She was as still as a mouse, she thought, but then his head ached, poor fellow! So she went out and sat in the shade of the house among her morning-glories, while the hens walked about with their wings down and their tongues lolling out, trying to cool themselves. The black-burnt prairie seemed to send up shafts of heat to the copper-coloured sky.

A man rode up to the bars, and for one moment Olive's heart stood still. She feared it might be Mr. Cotterell, whom she had not seen since the day at the spring, now some weeks past. It was not Mr. Cotterell, however, but one of the settlers from the other side of Cotton Wood Creek. He came forward with his bridle-rein over his arm, his horse following, head down.

"Wal, how'd you 'uns git 'long with that pesky fire?" he observed, without any preliminary greeting. He was a Missouri man, and they often prided themselves on their rudeness. It was their way of showing their independence.

"Good morning, Mr. Owen," said Olive, who knew the man quite well. "We have escaped all right, thank you. I hope you were not injured?" She was extra careful in her manner, as the politeness for two had all to be furnished by herself.

"Yer hain't been burnt out I see. You all's mighty silly anyhow. Why in thunder didn't yer back-fire before? 'Tain't agin' yer principles, is it?" Mr. Owen grinned under the impression that he was funny.

"We didn't back-fire, because we thought it wrong to start a fire in such a wind and let it possibly burn up our neighbours," said Olive stiffly.

"Then 'tis agin yer principles to back-fire, by Gosh! The boys was 'lowing as much over to Union Mills."

"It is against our principles to injure our neighbours. You don't object to that, Mr. Owen, do you?" said Olive.

"I reckon you'll git mighty tired o' them idees ef yer live long on the prairie," observed Mr. Owen.

"Seen ole man Cotterell lately?" he inquired suddenly, half shutting his green-grey eyes and looking at Olive intently.

She was somewhat surprised at the question, but knowing from experience how inquisitive the average settler is, she answered readily enough.

"No, I haven't seen him for a long time. Was he burnt out? I didn't know the fire had gone so far."

"I calkerlate he warn't tetched by the fire," said Mr. Owen, very slowly. He made long pauses between his remarks, during which he continued unremittingly the steady occupation of his life, namely, chewing tobacco. Olive began to feel impatient. She did not like to ask him into the house for fear of disturbing Ezra, so she sat down again in her chair, and pointing to a log of wood which lay near and seated on which he could still hold his horse, she asked him to take a seat also. Mr. Owen sat down with a grunt.

"Never seed ony pusson so sot on posies as you 'uns be," he observed conversationally.

"Yes, I am very fond of flowers. They make the house more home-like, I think. The prairie is very bare looking," replied Olive politely.

"Yer ole man oughter rared his house t'other side the Gully, an' further down yon'er. This hyar 'ull be powerful col' when we git col' snaps in Jan'ary. Yer dunno nothin' 'bout things in this hyar all-fired 'Fection City," said Mr. Owen, looking around him in criticism.

"Perhaps not," said Olive, rather nettled, "but we know how to mind our own business."

Mr. Owen did not feel one whit abashed. He was far too near akin to the pachyderms for Olive's delicate little shafts to have any effect on him. Another long silence followed, and Olive began to wonder if Owen was like that man from Jacksonville, who came to see them once and stayed four hours, during which time he made only two remarks and they possessed no particular interest. The man and his stony silence had driven her nearly wild, until she reflected how much more awful it would have been had she been obliged to entertain him with conversation. A recollection of this visitation and a dread born of that recollection began to invade her mind. Mr. Owen, however, was not going to stay for four hours, and he was going to make a remark of very particular interest, a remark that would quickly scatter all Olive's other ideas. He delivered it slowly and with the monotonous enunciation which proclaimed him a Missouri man.

"The boys is hout huntin' down ole man Cotterell."

"What!" exclaimed Olive turning very white. Then, steadying her voice as well as she could she said, "Why are they hunting him?"

"To cotch him," replied her visitor concisely.

"But what for?" asked Olive, looking at him with wide eyes of horror. She knew only too well what hunting down a man portended.

"Wal, there's bin a shootin' over to his house, an' one o' thim boys o' Mills is shot, shot dead. Cotterell done it. And now he's gone an' run off. The boys they 'lowed Cotterell best be hung this time. Las' time he was let off. He won't be agin, you bet."

"How do you know he has shot young Mills? What evidence have you of it?" asked Olive in terror, yet she could not help pressing the man to tell her, although each word was like a stab.

He gave a silent inward laugh as if his thoughts were facetious. "Evidence an' enough," he said. "Jake Mills' body with a bullet through his heart. Yer can't git nothin' plainer in the way of evidence than that, I reckon."

"But how do you know it was Mr. Cotterell shot him?" asked Olive.

"Damn my eyes! but yer mus' be a nateral-born fool, Mis' Weston. Jake Mills were foun' on Cotterell's lan'. Who else could ha' done it? Besides, he did, an' that's a fac' anyhow."

"I think it is perfectly monstrous," burst out Olive, trembling with agitation. "I never heard of a wickeder thing. Here is this man you have decided to hang, and you don't even know if he has done the thing you accuse him of. If that is what you call prairie law and justice I can only say I never heard of a more sinful and unjust law. Black savages couldn't do worse."

"Mos' like the boys will let him hev a trial, ef he's partic'lar sot on't. That won't si'nify nothin'," said Mr. Owen, again surveying Olive through the narrow aperture of his half-closed eyes, and again applying himself to his habitual occupation with vigour. She looked at him with a face in which horror and disgust struggled for mastery.

"If this horrid murder is committed by your neighbours, Mr. Owen, I shall think that prairie men are a disgrace to civilization," said Olive.

"We prairie folks ain't partic'lar sot on civilization," remarked Mr. Owen with affability.

"I hope you'll never catch him," said Olive, with a sound very like a sob in her voice.

"The boys they 'lowed you'uns was mighty good frien's o' his'n, an' he'd a mos' likely come this hyar way to make for the Pottawattamie 'fore we'uns could cotch him. That's why I come 'long ter look for him hyar," observed Mr. Owen, rising and putting his head under his saddle flap in order to tighten up the girth a couple of holes.

"Oh, you've come here to spy out, have you?" said Olive, in passionate anger. "Why didn't you say so at first, and ask the question like a man, and not come sneaking around? Do you want to hunt all over the house and see if we've got anybody hidden away?"

"No," said Owen slowly. "Guess that'll do. I ain't agoin' ter hunt roun'. We ain't no great shakes at bein' fine folks out hyar on the prairie, but we allers takes the word of a lady, by Gosh. You said you hain't seen nothin' o' ole man Cotterell, guess that'll do for the boys. Mornin'."

Mr. Owen rode away, feeling that in the contest of politeness that morning he had certainly scored off Mrs. Weston with her stuck-up Eastern ways.

Olive was in an agony of doubt and terror. That the boys were out hunting for Cotterell was, she knew, but the preliminary to his death, if they caught him. The boys seldom or never let off any one they caught, so she gathered from the stories she had heard of their doings in time past. What was she to do in this difficult dilemma? Should she tell Ezra?

Under ordinary circumstances her first impulse would have been to go straight to her husband with the story she had heard, but in this instance she felt that such a course would be impossible. She knew that Ezra was jealous of Mr. Cotterell, he had betrayed his feelings more than once, and in her heart she knew that few men can be just towards the man who arouses their jealousy. Her husband was a very just man, and could, more than any one she knew, put himself in the place of others and see what was right and what was wrong. But in this instance it was not justice Olive wanted, it was justice that she feared. Although she spoke bravely enough to Owen, a terrible fear lurked in her breast that the evidence, though ludicrously deficient by the rules of procedure that obtain in old established communities, was quite sufficient to convince a prairie jury. Ezra would not sit on a hanging jury, nor would he be a party to catching Mr. Cotterell, but his sense of justice and what was due to the principles professed at Perfection City might carry him no further than this passively inactive point? Would he assist Cotterell to escape? Guilty or not, that was what Olive wanted, and to help in such an undertaking, she felt sure, was what her husband might very well refuse to do.

Was Cotterell guilty? Olive debated this point anxiously in her mind. She knew he went armed, but so did many other men. In fact, to be armed was the rule on the prairie. The doctrine of non-resistance was one of the least understood tenets of the Pioneers at Perfection City, and was observed by nobody else on the prairie. Even Brother Wright, as we have seen—though Olive was quite unaware of this—had granted to himself a special indulgence in this matter. So the mere fact of Mr. Cotterell's always having his revolver in his belt did not really count for anything, one way or the other. He had always been so gentle and so chivalrous in his manner to her, she found it difficult to force her mind to keep hold of the fact that he was a very passionate man. Everyone said so, and she knew, too, that the Mills' were a bad lot, drunken quarrelsome men, who, as Ezra said, combined in their character all the vices of the prairie and preserved none of its virtues. How easy it would be for a proud, passionate man like Mr. Cotterell to bring his revolver into a heated argument with Jake Mills, who might be mad with drink. But surely such a shooting was not murder according to prairie-law. In her distress Olive found herself falling back upon the probable laxity of that very prairie justice which a short time before she had so scornfully characterised to Owen.

The "boys" who were hunting Cotterell were, as Olive well knew, the most relentless men on the prairie, regular settlers who had found by experience that the only way to keep order was to keep it with their own right hands. They had hung several horse-thieves lately, and had declared they were going to put a stop to the "shooting round promiscuous" of the younger blades. They were not unjust men, but they were hasty, and were moreover already terribly prejudiced against Cotterell.

Having decided that it was best not to tell Ezra what she had heard, Olive was immediately assailed with a hundred doubts. Suppose Mr. Cotterell came to them in his extremity, should she try to conceal him? But how utterly impossible to do so without the co-operation of her husband! The mere attempt to do such a thing might involve her in difficulties without being of any use to the unhappy man himself. Then there was Madame. Should she appeal to her for help? Her heart revolted from such a course. After their last meeting, when they had interchanged hot words on the subject of this very man, Olive felt it was impossible to ask Madame's aid or to tell her anything about it. Then there was no one, and Olive resolved to keep the secret of what she had heard, hoping that something might turn up which would justify her action, or at least make any further action unnecessary. Thus do people often put off on the shoulders of chance the burden of a decision which taxes too much their powers of forecasting events. It was a heavy secret to keep to herself, and her face looked white and scared as she entered the kitchen on tip-toe to see how Ezra felt. He roused up as she came in.

"I am better now, little woman," he said in answer to her inquiries. "The pain is all gone. I will get up and begin to stir around again."

He went out with her and with the keenness which is soon a habit with a prairie man, he noticed the hoof-marks of Owen's horse, where it had stamped rather briskly, owing to the flies.

"Who has been here? Those are fresh," he said, pointing to the marks.

"That man from over beyond Cotton Wood Creek was here a little while ago, Owen is his name: you know the man," said Olive, with a beating heart.

"Cattle-hunting after the fire, I suppose. Were they burnt out yesterday?" asked Ezra, with slight show of interest.

"No, I believe not, he did not say. He sneered at the Pioneers for not having safe-guarded themselves, heedless of the welfare of the other settlers, so I suppose he had been betimes with his back-firing, at least if he lives up to his principles," remarked Olive.

"It is too late to go and hunt for our horses," said Ezra, "and I feel too tired to start out on foot after them. They may very well be five miles away by this time. Did you ask Owen if he had seen them?"

"No, I never thought of doing so."

"Don't forget always to ask everyone if they have seen your horses whenever they are out on the prairie: it is one of the golden rules of prairie life," said Ezra, tapping her chin.

"But he wouldn't have known Queen Katharine and Rebel even if he did happen to meet them,"' objected Olive. "How could he know one pair of strange horses from another?"

"Bless your sweet eyes, Owen knows every horse and cow belonging to his neighbours for a radius of ten miles from his house, at the very least. Telling a neighbour where his cattle are, is the only rule of politeness known to many of them, and they are punctilious about it," said Ezra laughing.

"I wish I had known that, because I found him deficient in many of the rules I have been taught," said Olive. "Possibly he found me as lacking, according to his estimate."

Ezra did not go out to hunt for the horses the next morning as he had intended. Other work, which seemed more important, turned up for him. Brother Wright came that same evening to arrange about it.

"Good evening, friends," he said. "I trust you are both rested after yesterday. It was a hard day and a harder night. Brother Ezra, you did splendidly."

"We were much alarmed for the safety of Perfection City: I don't think it is ever likely to be in greater danger," said Ezra.

"No, I suppose, not from the outside," said Wright.

"And we are not likely to be set on fire from the inside, are we?" observed Ezra with a laugh.

"Accidents may happen," said Olive.

"Even in the best regulated communities," added Brother Wright. "However, what I came to talk about was the future, and not the past. We've got two good loads of corn ready, it ought to be sold at once in Mapleton. We'll get top price. I stepped into Madame's as I came along, and she agreed with me. We must sell at once. Brother Dummy has got his waggon loaded up ready to start. It is a marvel how much that man does get through in the way of work. Well, the question is, who will go with the corn? Brother Dummy must drive his own team, because no other man could manage that black horse for half an hour. Biting Bill would kick the waggon into match-wood in two minutes, if any of us attempted to touch his reins. I wonder whether it is the absolutely silent driving which cows him? You are out and out the best one for attending to business of any here. Madame thinks it would be well for you to go, and so do I."

"I am quite ready," replied Ezra. "But my horses are both out on the prairie. I turned them loose after the fire to let them run off to the Creek, as I had no time to put them up and feed them. To-day I did not feel able to hunt after them."

"Well, suppose you take my team, and I will find your horses for you to-morrow. Will that do?"

"All right, then I'll go to Mapleton."

"The corn is already shucked, it won't take half an hour to load up. You and I will do it while the horses are feeding. You ought to get off by six, I will feed the horses at five."

Each spoke of *his* horses and *his* waggons much in the same way as an artillery officer speaks of his guns. There were three pairs of horses in the Community, and, in theory at least, everyone was equally free to use them, but experience showed that that sort of handling did not suit horses, who do better if left always in the care of the same persons. Therefore it came about that Brother Dummy always had Biting Bill, since no one else could manage the brute, and Ezra generally had Queen Katharine and Rebel, while

Brother Wright kept the greys. Now these animals, although common property, were invariably spoken of by their drivers as *theirs*, for the use of certain familiar phrases, which to the outsider might seem to denote the idea of private property, came naturally to their lips. It is often more difficult to change habits of speech than laws of property. Reformers who start out to alter the whole course of modern ideas and to rearrange the world according to a plan of their own devising, would do well to meditate upon this peculiarity and see what it points to. Surely so slight a thing as a word might easily be eradicated from human speech, and yet how difficult it is to do so. But the point to consider is that the pertinacity, which shows itself in modes of expression, may very well exist in just as strong a form in habits of thought and feeling. The Pioneers, like others of that sort, passed over and disregarded such expressions as " my horse," " my waggon," and " your plough," not apparently recognizing that the expressions denoted a habit of thought that might very easily strike at the very root of their institution. They were communists, as Olive had said, in bits of this and scraps of that, but the old leaven of individualism was there still among them, only dormant. The Pioneers never expected that the leaven would again become an active principle. Like other people, they were unable to see into the future, and therefore rejoiced in their escape from the perils of the prairie fire and considered that they had no further danger to apprehend for this winter at least. The sea was smooth and the sky was serene, so to speak, and they did not perceive the sunken rocks that lay in the track of their experimental bark.

# CHAPTER XV.

### IN QUEST OF NEWS.

OLIVE was early astir the next morning, in order to see her husband off and also to provide him with food in ample abundance to last him for the trip. He carried a plentiful store of dried beef, a portable commodity much in request on the prairie. The old trappers had showed the settlers how to make it, and the trappers had acquired the art from the Indians. Dried beef is precisely what its name indicates. It is raw beef, somewhat salted, and then dried in the sun until it is like a piece of solid leather. It has to be cut into thin slices across the grain before the stoutest teeth can make the slightest impression upon it. It may be also cooked in a batter of eggs for the dainty, but has only to be sliced up with a jack-knife to be eaten by the average teamster on the prairie. Besides the dried meat and plenty of corn-bread, Ezra had milk in a bottle and one of Olive's wedding presents to eat, namely, a tin of peaches. He travelled therefore in extreme luxury. He set off along with Brother Dummy just as the sun was rising, and the canvas covers of the waggons showed for a long time as two moving white specks as they slowly crept across the blackened landscape, finally disappearing behind the Mounds some twelve miles to the west of Perfection City.

Olive remained alone at home with Napoleon Pompey and Diana to keep her company, until Ezra should return in four days' time. It was only with great reluctance that he had consented to this. He did not at all like the idea of her remaining alone in the house. As usual, when it came to Olive doing what the ordinary prairie settler's wife did as a matter of course, Ezra's love took fright. He urged her to go and stay at Madame's house, she would be more than welcome, he declared, in fact it seemed to him almost necessary that she should go, and he insisted strongly upon the plan. Olive was as strongly opposed to it. Why couldn't she stay in her own house? She would much prefer it, so as to be on hand to feed the chickens and milk the cows and generally see to things. Besides, she felt quite sure she would be vastly in Madame's way. Ezra combated this position vigorously. Olive could not be in anyone's way, even if she tried. Moreover, was not Madame a communist like the rest of them, and she would be only too pleased to take Olive into her home as she had already done into her heart. His spouse made no comment, except a mental one, to this argument, but reiterated her preference for staying at home. It would only be three days or four at most, and she would be very busy. Ezra hinted at possible danger if it were known she was alone in the house.

"But I won't be alone: there is Napoleon Pompey for one and Diana for two. Surely between so stout a pair nothing on earth can happen to me," she said, smiling at his anxious face.

"I don't feel easy about you," said Ezra, looking at her with mournful eyes. "I never left you alone before, and it suddenly seems to me a most portentous thing."

"Why, you dear silly old thing!" exclaimed Olive, "I do believe you'll have omens next, and will look into tea-cups to see if it is a propitious moment for the success of this undertaking. I never knew you 'take on' like this before."

"I never did so, but it is all because I love you, dear. I quite understand what it means, to be foolish with love. I used not to know what it was. I wonder do women ever feel the same as we men do?"

"Women, my dear, are sent into this world for the express purpose of making men do what they ought and not be silly," said Olive severely. "Now I know you'll have the feed for the horses all right, but remember the feed for yourself is in this basket, everything you'll want, and there is salt for the boiled eggs."

When the hurry of getting the waggons off was over, Olive sat down to think, and immediately there rose up before her the image of a hunted man flying for his life. In some ways it was a relief that Ezra was gone, she would not have to be constantly making an effort to hide the real anxiety in her mind. Then she thought of Ezra and of his great and boundless devotion to her, and the words Madame had spoken in her wrath rose up before her and rebuked her. Were they true? Had she hidden her real nature from her husband before her marriage? She had never meant to do so, but in their long pre-nuptial conversations it had not appeared to her that she and Ezra were so different in their views of life and its duties as perhaps was now the case. He certainly had told her of the experiment of Perfection City, and she had accepted him and the experiment together because they were indissoluble. She of herself would never have initiated the communistic idea; but then there was nothing wonderful in that, woman never do initiate anything, they only follow some man's lead with more or less enthusiasm and intelligence.

Were she to have expressed her own private predilection, it certainly would have been for a little home of her own on the usual lines, which little home it would have been her pride and her pleasure to make as beautiful as she could. Olive did not possess a large and speculative mind, capable of vast dreamy projects, whose limitless possibilities were in imagination not checked by small practical obstacles. On the contrary, it was the tendency of her intellect to perceive those obstacles with startling clearness, and to demonstrate, by a few biting truisms, the impossibility of turning the dreamy vastnesses to use. She was neither hard-headed nor dull-headed, but hers was a practical nature, very much jarred by idle vapourings, and above all she was kept in the straight path of common sense by her keen appreciation of the ridiculous.

This faculty enabled her to perceive how often reformers run off the track of common sense, and while pinning their faith to one particular little tenet which they constitute the corner-stone of their philosophy, lose sight of the whole world beyond. Olive possessed in a high degree the sense of proportion, which in a true reformer is generally absent. When Ezra with his cultivated mind and really fine intellect, talked to her of the reforming of the present type of civilization, and briefly sketched out what he hoped would be the result of the introduction of the communistic idea into life, she could not help remarking that he used very much the same expressions, and seemed animated by very much the same hopes, as those indulged in by one of the dietetic reformers she knew in Smyrna, who promised all the glories of the golden age to mankind if the human race would only give up the baneful practices of eating meat and of cooking vegetables!

And every few minutes, across the mirror of her reflections, there came a shadow of a desperate man spurring on a jaded horse. Olive could not shake off a sense of impending disaster, but unlike Ezra, who attributed his melancholy to his great love for Olive and a vague, unreasoning dread of something happening to her in his absence, she knew quite well what she feared and why.

As the morning wore on, Olive began to feel it impossible to remain quietly at home in the midst of her anxiety. She must go out and hear what news there was, or at all events she must learn if there was any news. Resolved not to hold any communication with Madame other than what was publicly necessary —for between the two there was now maintained a sort of armed neutrality—she decided to call at the blacksmith's, as Brother Green was in the way of most of the gossip, if gossip is a term that could be rightly applied to the feeble and intermittent stream of prairie news that trickled through the smithy. Brother Green was a silent, self-absorbed man who worked steadily and brought much personal devotion into the project of Perfection City. He was a lonely man, a widower, and to judge by appearances a disappointed man as well. He was surprised to see Sister Olive, and very pleased, but could not shake hands as he was very dirty, and she looked so brightly clean. Having wiped a wooden bench with his leather apron and again with the sleeve of his shirt, he invited her to be seated. Brother Green was welding some iron, and Olive waited until the operation was concluded and the plough-hook made before she talked to him. Meanwhile she watched with interest the white glowing fire and the pulpy white-hot iron-bar, helplessly bending over at the end like a piece of half boiled molasses candy.

"I felt so lonesome, I thought I would come out and talk to someone," she said, by way of excuse for a first visit. "Diana isn't a bit of company when you feel really lonesome. Ezra is gone for four days, did you know?"

Diana had cocked one ear at the mention of her name, but had speedily uncocked it again on becoming satisfied that nothing in the way of excitement was at hand.

"Yes, I suppose you do feel lonely," said Brother Green slowly, as he seated himself on his anvil and crossed his brawny arms. "I've been used to it for so long, I have almost forgotten how anything else feels."

Olive looked kindly at him. "Are you ever homesick, and do you ever wish you had stayed in England? It must be very different from here."

"Very," said Brother Green gazing with a faraway sort of look through the large forge door out over the shimmering prairie. He suddenly seemed to see rolling hills with oak woods tufting their slopes, and a deep valley, where blue curling smoke ascended in high spirals, and a church steeple rose from among elms, and jackdaws croaked around the steeple. He put his head a little on one side, almost as if he would catch more distinctly the hoarse croak of the jackdaws, or maybe the first sound of the bell which hung in the steeple and used to ring on Sundays.

"Yes," he said, as this picture faded away and the prairie returned in its place, "there can't be much greater differences in the world than between Perfection City and the little village in Sussex, where I was born."

"Which do you like best, Brother Green?" asked Olive a little thoughtlessly.

"I don't expect ever to be as unhappy again as I was in that pretty little village," said Brother Green, and Olive remembered that she had been told he had lost a young wife in his youth. She felt sorry for him, and regretted having touched upon an old wound that still could throb with pain.

"Have you heard any news lately? Has anybody been to the forge? You are always the first to hear news," said she quickly, desiring to change the subject.

"A man from down south passed this morning."

"Did he?" said Olive anxiously, "what did he say?"

"He said the fire was just bellowing its way towards Fort Scott, and had done a good deal of damage one way or another. It was one of the hottest they ever had and the hardest to stop. It crossed one of the South Fork Creeks and got into the broken land round Osage."

"We had a very narrow escape ourselves," said Olive, feeling remarkably little interest in the fire. "Did he say anything else? Who was he?"

"A stranger, I never saw him before. No, he didn't say anything else, except to tell me that he calkerlated Britishers were mos'ly fools and couldn't do a day's work 'gain 'Mericans, no matter what it were, rail-splitting or tobacco-chawin'."

Brother Green gave a deep gentle laugh, like the distant boom of a waterfall hidden among trees.

"Don't you think these prairie folk are most conceited?" asked Olive, in some scorn.

"No, not more than other people, Sister," replied Brother Green somewhat unexpectedly, "they only say what they think with remarkable frankness."

"But that is conceit," persisted Olive.

"I am not certain that it is more conceited to say what you think, than to think your thoughts in silence, and be consumed with a vast contempt for all the world. We are a conceited people too."

"I thought the English prided themselves on not being conceited," said Olive.

"We pride ourselves on showing no feeling of conceit and if possible on showing no feeling on any other subject either. If an Englishman's heart were skinned, I think it would weigh up pretty much the same as an American's. The difference lies in the tongue only."

"Is that so?" said Olive.

"Yes, this morning, for instance, that man informed me that he was a better man than I, and that his country could lick mine. Well, in my heart I knew he was wrong on both points, and that the precise contrary was the fact. As far as essentials go, I think we were pretty equal in the contest of conceit."

"But you didn't tell him what you thought," remarked Olive.

"No, that was the difference of tongue, not of heart," replied Brother Green.

"I didn't know you were so severe in your criticisms and judgments. I wonder much what you really think of Perfection City," said Olive, looking at him curiously. She had never particularly noticed him hitherto, and had not realized that he could have a store of knowledge of many things which lay far outside her experience.

"I think Perfection City will do good," said Brother Green with conviction.

"Do you, and why?" asked Olive.

"Any honest human effort to benefit the world and raise mankind does good," said Brother Green.

"But people have done such different things and all from a desire to do what seemed to them good," objected Olive with feminine vagueness.

"I consider they have done good if their purpose was single-hearted," maintained Brother Green.

"They didn't succeed in doing what they aimed at very often, at all events," observed Olive, "something quite different came out of their endeavours from what they had expected."

"Nevertheless, if they honestly tried, then that very trying was of itself good."

"Do you think Perfection City will do the good the Pioneers expect, or will something quite different come out of it too?"

"I think Perfection City will be the means of teaching a valuable lesson," said Brother Green cordially.

"Do you think it is any use to try to change the world and its ideas?"

"If anyone has a truth let him preach it fearlessly. Who can foretell the moment when the world will listen and when it is ready to profit by your example."

Olive longed to ask him what he thought of Madame, but dared not do so. She felt a little afraid before this simple-minded man, with his fervent, childlike faith and his sad and lonely life. Belief in Perfection City might be his only comfort now, shut off as he was from the joys of home and family, she would do nothing to lessen his belief and make him more lonely still. For what is more lonely than the heart out of which a faith has departed never to return? So she bade him good-bye, and then seeing Aunt Ruby's chimney giving off the cheerful smoke of habitation, she turned her steps thither. Olive walked slowly along, for it was very hot indeed with a dry suffocating heat that made exertion somewhat irksome, and Diana, the discreet, followed dutifully behind her.

Aunt Ruby, as has been already hinted, had surrounded herself with a large family of chickens of all ages, to whose wants it was her great duty to attend. She had a rare hand for chickens, and could pick up the most spasmodic specimen and turn it upside down and examine it for the gapes without hurting it in the least. Her driving of the hens to roost was an exhibition of the talent of generalship worthy of a wider field. No screamings nor scurryings, no rushings madly hither and thither, took place, and above all no sticks were used in the ceremony: Aunt Ruby merely took her skirts gently at the side in each hand, and said "Shoo! Shoo!" in a soothing voice, while at the same time she slightly oscillated the folds of her skirt. The hens appeared hypnotized by the action, and no matter how eagerly they might be pursuing the afternoon fly, they would at once settle down into a conversational chuck-a-chu and begin forthwith to meander towards the hen-roost.

Aunt Ruby's numerous hens and chickens were all in the yard and around the wood-pile, seeking in an aimless over-fed fashion after chance insects, when suddenly, without a moment's warning, the devil was upon them according to the gallinaceous imagination. The devil was possessed of four paws, a most terrifying bark, and a mouth that seemed to the affrighted birds to be on the point of devouring each one especially and individually. The dog flew hither and thither, and so did the chickens, and so did the tail feathers.

"Diana! Bad dog, down, down!" screamed Olive, rushing to the rescue, while Aunt Ruby with shrill cry and a broom-stick appeared in the door-way. Never before or since did a more tempestuous guest appear at Aunt Ruby's house. Full a quarter of an hour of gentle "shoo-shooings" to the hens, interspersed with smart whippings to Diana, elapsed before quiet was restored, and the ladies could even begin their visit together. Even then there was a sort of nervous tension on Aunt Ruby's part, which prevented her thorough enjoyment of the opportunity for a gossip. Her attention was distracted by Diana, who lay with lamb-like docility at Olive's feet and slept the sleep of the just.

"I wouldn't keep a dawg roun' nohow," said Aunt Ruby eyeing the delinquent sternly. "I'd mos' as lief hev a rattlesnake. I shouldn't never sleep easy in my bed won'erin' an' won'erin' what the pesky crittur 'ud do nex'."

"I know that Diana is very naughty now, but she is only a puppy, and she'll get sense by and bye, and it is so nice to have something that is your own and loves you, and doesn't care for any body else, you know," observed Olive somewhat rashly.

"Wal, I reckon you'll hev a sight o' trouble 'long o' that dawg 'fore you learn it the rights o' people, let alone teachin' it community idees," said Aunt Ruby.

"No, you can't teach a dog communistic notions,

thank goodness," observed Olive, patting the sinful Diana.

"Reckon you ain't partic'ler sot on the idees of Perfection City," said the old lady, looking at her visitor with bright twinkling eyes. "I allow there be a p'int or two we'll hev to consider over agin at 'Sembly. We are gettin' on too fas' fur this here prairie folk, they hain't got the sense to un'erstan' all o' our highest principles. Guess while there's Injuns roun' we hed better jes' hol' back a mite 'bout non-resistance."

"Oh," said Olive, who had never given any attention to this point, being as indifferent as the wives of strong men usually are. "I never heard a word about Indians. Are there any about?"

"Not as I hearn on special. But there's Injuns and worse nor Injuns in the world, an' I reckon we'd better take that p'int up at 'Sembly and see if we can't do su'thin' to make things a bit straight," said Aunt Ruby in language that was vaguely enough expressed to serve in the highest walks of diplomacy.

"Oh, I dare say," replied Olive carelessly, "some very excellent reason could be devised to excuse a departure from any one of the Perfection City principles, which seem more difficult to manage in practice than on paper. They are all pretty new, and of course can't be expected to be as useful in all the difficult circumstances of life as principles which have stood the test of time."

"Dear me, suz!" exclaimed Aunt Ruby admiringly. "How gran' you kin talk! Deal sight finer nor Brother Wright. Why don't you hold forth in 'Sembly? I'd liefer hear you nor any on 'em. I'm jes' 'bout tired o' listenin' to Brother Wright. Lard! how he do love to hear his own voice! Hens is jes' like that too, they'll talk an' talk till you're mos' crazy, an' they hain't nothin' to say, on'y jes' to cackle an' hear themselves talk."

Olive agreed with Aunt Ruby, but hardly dared to express her opinion in all its force. Therefore she turned the conversation by inquiring had she ever heard anything about lynch-law and about its being put into practice in their neighbourhood?

"Course I hev, an' hearn o' hangin' too."

"Do Perfection City principles uphold hanging?" asked Olive.

"Guess not," was the reply.

"No matter if it was for murder?"

"Wal, I don't see as we could ever be called upon to settle that p'int, 'cause no 'Fectionist could ever be a murderer no how," said Aunt Ruby.

"But suppose an outsider who had shot a man, even if it was not a real bad murder, came to us for protection, would they help him, do you think?" asked Olive.

"Wal, I never hearn that debated at the 'Sembly, but I reckon Perfection City don't lay out to hide folks as has killed a feller critter. It don't 'pear to me as how we was called upon to min' anyone 'cept our own selves, an' we hed best keep clear 'way o' them sort o' folks. That's pretty nigh my 'pinion, an' I guess it's mos' folks too as hes a mite o' common sense."

Olive was fain to confess to herself that in all probability Aunt Ruby did fairly express the collective opinion of Perfection City. They had only enough righteousness for themselves, and, like a ship already short of provisions, could not help another vessel, even though it might be flying the Union Jack upside down and showing all the other flags of acute distress recognized in the naval code of signals. Had Aunt Ruby heard of anything concerning a horse-thief who was supposed to be somewhere around, inquired Olive with a view to eliciting information, but she only elicited feminine alarms in overwhelming abundance.

"Do tell! Land o' liberty! Was there horse-thieves 'bout? What a pity Brother Ezry an' Brother Dummy was both gone jes' now: they might meet in 'Sembly right away an' discuss the p'int o' non-resistance an' buy revolvers next time anyone went to Union Mills. Horse-thieves was mos' as bad as Injuns, an' if it was lawful an' right to defen' yourself 'gainst Injuns as was ign'rant savages as never hed Christian teachin', it couldn't be wrong to look a'ter your hosses as was bought an' paid for by 'Fection City money."

Aunt Ruby was so convinced and loquacious upon this subject and upon the aspect of the case as presented to her mind by her terrors, that Olive heartily regretted her question, and began to try and do away with the effects of it as far as possible. It was only a vague report she averred, and Olive herself had not the slightest idea that there were horse-thieves about. Upon the strength of this assurance Aunt Ruby, somewhat comforted, allowed her attention to be engaged by other topics of conversation. She was much distressed that she could not persuade her visitor to stay all the rest of the day and have a real good soul-satisfying talk, but Olive declared she must go home and see to her own chickens, an argument that appealed very strongly to Aunt Ruby's maternal instincts.

A difficulty arose as to how Diana was to be decently conducted out through the yard.

"I'd mos' as soon hev to conten' with a roarin' lion as that pup," remarked Aunt Ruby as the difficulty presented itself to her mind in an acute form.

"If I could get her past without seeing the hens and chickens she would be all right," said Olive, who of course had no whip, regarding meditatively the dog, who of course had no collar.

"Wal, that 'ud do, I guess, sort o' take her out o' the way o' temptation," said Aunt Ruby, surveying Diana with an anxious eye. "I kin give you an ole caliker skirt o' mine, an' you kin tie up her head in that reg'lar tight, so as she wouldn't see ne'er a hen this side o' Christmas, 'less you took it off."

This seemed a hopeful arrangement; so the "caliker skirt" was brought, and the misguided Diana, under the impression that a brand new game was on foot, allowed her head to be hidden in the folds of the skirt. Olive then led her to the door, but Diana objected, not seeing where the joke came in for her; and as soon as she found that she was ignominiously tied into the dreadful skirt, her rage was boundless. In an instant she wrenched herself free from Olive's guiding hand. She then commenced a wild career around the yard backwards, swaying this way and that in the most ghastly and unlooked-for manner.

The hens and chickens no sooner beheld this portent than with one universal squawk of horror they betook themselves to places of safety under the corn-crib and into the cracks of the wood-pile, whence they could not again be coaxed for many hours. Diana meanwhile continued her fearsome course and ere long came into violent contact with the chicken-tub, a large receptacle with loose wooden cover where various sorts of food suitable for fowls were collected together, first thinned with water and then thickened into a glutinous mass by intermixture of corn-meal. Into this tub Diana sat with extreme violence and then rolled over. Olive caught her as she was emerging from the chicken-tub and by uncovering her eyes restored her to reason. Aunt Ruby, speechless with indignation, and Olive, equally speechless with laughter, then set to work with two big spoons to scrape the chicken food from the ground and from the hind quarters of the dog. Diana, now at peace with all the world, wagged her tail benevolently during this process, and soon specked Olive over with corn-meal, potatoes, scraps of peelings, and bits of greens, until she looked as if she had been out in a snow-storm as severe in character as it was diversified in composition. When this job was over Aunt Ruby arose and straightened her old back with a groan.

"Wal, I guess I would a deal sight sooner hev a rattlesnake to look a'ter than a dawg," she observed.

Olive, apologetic, departed along with the unrepentant Diana, and together they returned homewards.

## CHAPTER XVI.

#### HORSE THIEVES.

OLIVE spent a few quiet hours at home along with Diana, and then took supper in company with Napoleon Pompey, whose manners at table were now all that could be desired. Indeed, the negro in this connection easily takes a higher polish than might be expected: he prides himself on being punctilious in all the forms and phrases of the best white society he has ever come in contact with, and being highly imitative, is quickly trained. Given a white boy and a black boy of similar ages and depths of ignorance, the black one will more quickly tame into a seemingly quiet human being, while very frequently the same vanity which prompts a negro to be over-zealous in the use of "please" and "thank you" will cause the white boy to act roughly and assert his independence by extravagances of rude behaviour. Napoleon Pompey was magnificently polite to "Mis' Ollie," whom he adored, and for whom he was ready even to work: that is to make the greatest sacrifice possible to a negro lad of twelve. He never forgot to carry in wood for her or to pick up chips in generous quantity for the lighting of the afternoon fire, and he collected abundance of corn-cobs and had them duly dried in the sun ready at her hand in case she was in sudden want of a hot fire. When working for Ezra, Napoleon Pompey reverted to his natural black standard of diligence and shirked as much as he possibly could, lying down in fence-corners to sleep like a shiny black lizard when he should have been stripping corn, but he never shirked "Mis' Ollie's" work. She didn't scold the lad, but ruled him by her gentleness and her beauty, and he fell into meekest subjection to her.

Olive always tried to talk with Napoleon Pompey at meals, even when Ezra was there, being anxious to make him feel at his ease and happy in their presence; and to-day being alone with him she thought she might get some information out of him on the subject which was weighing so heavily upon her mind.

"Napoleon Pompey, did you ever hear of their hunting down men on the prairie here?"

"Yo' bet, Mis' Ollie, I seed darkie what went to de hangin' ole man Howard. He done seed him hoisted over de tree slap up. He told me——"

"Hush!" said Olive sternly.

The young savage was abashed, he had meant no harm, but thought some pleasing details "o' de hangin'," which he himself had relished mightily, would prove equally acceptable to Olive's taste. She was disgusted to think that with all her teaching of the forms and symbols of politeness and gentle manners, which the young scamp had received with such docility, she had not really touched his heart at all: he was just a black savage, still rejoicing in vivid details of horrors and cruelty.

"Don't tell me," she said sternly, "that it is possible you could like to see a human being, a fellow creature, made in God's image, no matter how guilty he might be, put to death. It may be necessary, Napoleon Pompey, sometimes to hang men who have done wicked things, so as to prevent others from doing the same, but it is an awful thing, a sad and terrible sight. You would never wish to see it, Napoleon Pompey," said Olive solemnly.

"It 'ud be bully ter see 'um kickin' in de air wid rope roun' his neck," said Napoleon Pompey simply.

Olive turned white with disgust and left the kitchen, retiring with Diana to her own little private room. Napoleon Pompey, conscious of no shortcomings, cleared away the supper things very handily, washed the few dishes, set the candles upon the white deal table, and whistling in the innocence of his youthful heart went out to "walk roun'" and see that all was right, and the hen-house fastened up securely against possible visits from pole-cats, before he retired to his loft upstairs shortly after sun-down. Like the chickens, Napoleon Pompey went early to roost.

Conscious from the all-pervading stillness that the lad was gone to bed, Ollie returned to the kitchen, and her heart smote her as she saw two tallow candles in their tin candle-sticks placed on the table in convenient position for her to read, if such should be her wish. Poor Napoleon Pompey! Olive thought compassionately of what an affectionate boy he was, and of how it was not his fault if he still had savage tastes. Indeed, it was rather the fault of everybody else. His not very remote ancestors were unreclaimed African savages, and the career of those more immediate forefathers, whose lot had been cast in slavery down South, had not had an elevating tendency. It was wonderful, not that he still had savage tastes, but that he had got rid of so many of them. She was sorry that she had not been better able to control her feelings, and determined forthwith to institute a careful system of training with a view to leading him to the higher life by the shortest possible road. Having settled in her own mind a few of the more important lines upon which this training was to be conducted, Olive turned at last to her reading. But she could not keep her mind on her book, it kept wandering off in all sorts of directions, and at last took that of being frightened at the loneliness and stillness of the house. When so firmly combating the notion of being afraid to stay in the house during Ezra's absence, Olive had not realized how appalling the stillness would be. In the daytime there were multitudes of unregarded sounds, which went to make up the sum total of the idea of life and fellowship, but at night these had completely ceased, and she seemed to hear the stillness with awful intensity.

Then, too there were no shutters to the windows, which were, of course, open to let in the cool night air, and the thought suddenly came into Olive's mind of how exposed she really was, sitting there in the light of her candles, plainly to be seen, but unable to see out. A thought such as this needs but little time to grow into a veritable feeling of panic. She glanced at the black gaping windows and stared out into the measureless blackness beyond. At one moment she raised her hand to extinguish the candles and so to hide herself in the dark along with her fears, but she knew that would only make matters worse. She would see in her terrified imagination a hundred glaring eyes peering in through the window. She got up and walked about the room, trying by a little movement to throw off the oppressive sense of terror. Diana suddenly seemed to be interested in something, and raised her head and sniffed inquiringly, and her mistress, nervously awake to every sight or sound, looked anxiously around her and stopped in her uneasy walk. Diana arose and went to the door, and being a puppy wagged her tail effusively, then suddenly remembering that she ought to be a dog, barked with vehemence. Olive was ready to scream with nervous terror as she heard a step upon the slanting board which led up to the door and a second later a knock against the resounding wood. She stood spell-bound, unable to speak or move. Diana ceased barking, and looked with eager delight for the opening of the door.

"It is I, friends, let me come in," said a deep voice which thrilled Olive to the heart.

The door opened and Mr. Cotterell entered.

"Mr. Cotterell! What are you here for?" gasped Olive, as he came in and stood in the light, gaunt-eyed and hollow-cheeked.

"I am flying for my life, Mrs. Weston. The men are out hunting me down. I have come to ask your help. Where is your husband?"

"He is gone away to Mapleton."

"Ah!" said Cotterell, with a sigh that had some relief in the sound. "Then you will help me, won't you?"

"What have you done?" asked Olive, gazing at him in terror. He was wild-looking and so different from the charming gentleman she had known before.

"I've shot Jake Mills," he replied, without any attempt at dissimulation.

"Do you mean that you've murdered him?" gasped Olive, starting back from him.

"Good God! Mrs Weston, no. I've not murdered him, although he is dead by my hand. There's been a quarrel between us about some land he rented from me. He was a very low-bred fellow and violent, and I despised him, and—well, I said some harsh things to him about cheating the last time we met. He swore that he would pay me out. He came to my cabin the other day. I don't know how long ago, it seems a life-time. He was mad with drink and fury. I told him he was a hound. He whipped out his revolver and fired at me, but he was too tipsy to aim straight, his shots went wide of the mark. Well, I got my shot in, I was not drunk. That is how it was, Mrs. Weston. Upon my honour as a man, that is the exact truth. You would not call it murder, would you?"

"No, it was in self-defence. But why didn't you go and tell the neighbours at once? They understand that sort of thing on the prairie."

"Ah, there's just my hard luck. There was a brute of a negro who saw it all, a fellow I thrashed once for stealing and lying, and he said with such a meaning look, niggers were free men now, they could give evidence against white men now," said Cotterell in a voice of despair.

"Could not you silence him?" said Olive, "or make him tell the truth?"

"Yes, I could have silenced him easily enough, and I had my finger on the trigger to do it. But I sickened at the thought. I couldn't shoot him, although it was my life against his in all probability. I fled and he gave the alarm. I have no chance with these men around here to try me, and that negro to give his lying version of the fight. If it was a jury of men like your husband, it would be different, but these ignorant settlers are desperately prejudiced against me already as a foreigner, and because of several things in the past."

Olive thought of what her husband had said, and knew only too well that there was indeed much prejudice against the unhappy fugitive.

"What am I to do? You cannot stay here, Mr. Cotterell. They have already been looking for you. Mr. Owen was here yesterday afternoon."

"Did he tell you what I had done? Did he seem to consider it murder?"

"Yes, he did," said Olive in a whisper, not daring to remember what he had said should be Cotterell's punishment.

"But you don't look upon it in that light?" said he, wistfully.

"No, certainly not. It was a terrible misfortune that might happen to anybody, given the preliminary quarrel."

"Thank you," said Cotterell brokenly. "When a poor devil is being hunted down it is a comfort for him to find someone who can still believe in him, and I knew in my heart I could come to you for help when all else had abandoned me. I am starving, Mrs. Weston. I have eaten nothing for two days. Can you give me some food?"

"Poor fellow!" cried Olive, more struck perhaps by his bodily needs than by those of the mind. "Sit down here, I'll get you something in a jiffy. There is a good chicken-pie in the cellar."

She took a lantern and hurried off to the cellar which was under the house, but to which entrance was effected by an outside door. She brought him food and drink and sat by him as he ate ravenously, wolfishly.

"I must sleep or I shall never be able to hold out for the flight to-morrow. Let me lie here, will you, and wake me at mid-night. Will you do that for me? I must sleep. I have been hiding in the bottom-land of Cotton Wood Creek in the brushwood ever since I left home. I didn't dare to ride across the prairie with everybody out on account of the fire. I should have been seen by someone, even if I could have got clear of the fire. The hunt must be over now on this side of the county, and I may dare snatch a little sleep."

He flung himself down on the floor, and almost before Olive could fetch a pillow for his head he was in a deep sleep. She sat watching him and wondering what his life was. Somewhere away in England, perhaps, there was a blue-eyed girl waiting for him to come home, a girl whose blue eyes were getting dim with the tears she shed in that long long waiting. He was a very handsome man, with his yellow moustache and clear-cut features. His hat was off, leaving a sort of high-water mark plainly visible on his forehead, where the sun-burn ended and the smooth white skin showed upon his temples. The veins were marked in blue like a baby's, she remembered how Ezra had commented on these blue veins. She wondered who he was and why he came there to live, and all the while she watched the slow rise and fall of his chest as he breathed in his sleep with his right hand nervelessly holding his revolver. How he would start up and grip that weapon, and how his blue eyes would flash, if his pursuers should come upon him! He was a man that had a reputation for bravery even on the prairie, where few men were cowards. She thought of Prince Charlie and his wanderings, and all the stories she had read as a girl about that charming prince. Here was a fugitive seeking her aid, and she—well, she would act the part of Flora Macdonald. By the time it was midnight, Olive had worked herself into a most romantic frame of mind and was determined to help Mr. Cotterell at every hazard. She was not a person to do a thing by halves. She made a parcel of food for him out of the remains of the chicken-pie, and then, it being just midnight, she awoke him.

"Ah, Mrs. Weston, how can I ever show my gratitude to you? You are in veriest truth my guardian angel. I shall carry your image in my heart till I die," said Cotterell in his soft persuasive voice. "I should like to think that you had some memory of me."

"I shall not forget you, and shall pray that you may escape all dangers," said Olive gently.

"I have absolutely nothing that I can call my own. Would you accept this ring of mine as a token of my gratitude, and sometimes wear it in memory of me? When you look at it, think that somewhere in this weary world there is one heart that will be grateful to you until it ceases to beat."

He pulled a ring from his finger and put it into her hand. At the same time he stooped his tall form and softly kissed her forehead, saying: "God bless you!"

Olive's eyes were full of tears. "You must be going or it will be too late," she said with a sob.

"Yes, I must not tarry." He looked to his revolver, jerked his cartridge-case round into a more convenient position for rapidly opening it, and took up his hat.

"Where is your horse?"

"I hitched him to the bars."

"Then I will take the lantern and light you on your way. The night is very dark. Once on horseback you can ride by the light of the stars," said Olive.

"Yes, I'll shape my course for the Missouri border, if I can run the gauntlet of the people here. Once I reach a town and civilization I shall be all right."

They went to the bars, Olive holding her little

lantern which threw a feeble ray along the pathway.

"Great God!" cried Cotterell.

"Oh, what is it? Are they coming after you?" said Olive in alarm, dropping her lantern which instantly went out.

"My horse is gone!" said Cotterell, whose eyes were now becoming accustomed to the darkness. "I left him hitched here. He was a wild young colt, not half broken. See, this is the lariat-rope wrenched in two. I was a fool to trust to that rope, and a double-dyed fool to leave him here in the dark. But I was too hungry and too sleepy to think clearly of what I was doing. That sleep will cost me my life. I shall have plenty of time to sleep, aye forever, if daylight catches me here. Mrs. Weston will you add one more benefit to the many that have gone before? Will you give me a horse?"

"Oh, so gladly if I had one," said Olive, beginning to cry with grief and helplessness.

"Haven't you any horses?" asked Cotterell with a gasp.

"No. Ezra and Brother Huntley have taken two teams to Mapleton."

"Are there no more about the place?"

"Only our two that were out on the prairie. Brother Wright was to hunt for them."

"Did he find them?"

"I don't know. Perhaps he did."

"Then you must give me one of them. They are yours."

"They are not mine. Oh, I have not anything in this dreadful Community. It is horrible," wailed Olive.

"Don't, pray don't," said Cotterell feeling for her hand in the darkness and crushing it in a passionate grasp. "Come with me and help me get one."

"What! steal one of our horses?"

"Yes, God help me! if that must be the word. If I live, the Community shall have the horse's price ten times over. If I am hanged, put it down for the Recording Angel's tears. Come."

"The horses are not here. They are at Brother Wright's if anywhere."

"Can you find the way in the dark? Then come all the same."

He held her hand. Was it for fear lest she should turn back, or was it for some other reason? They walked in silence towards the Wrights' house, two dark shadows stealing through the blackness.

"Mr. Cotterell," whispered Olive with chattering teeth. "If anyone should come out of the house on account of the noise, don't fire. We are all non-resistants, you know, here, and he won't have a pistol." Olive had no knowledge of the plenary indulgence which Brother Wright had seen fit to bestow upon himself in this matter.

"Dear heart! don't fear," said Cotterell tenderly.

"I am a desperate man flying for his life, it is true, but I am not a dastard. No human being at Perfection City shall ever be hurt by my hand. They are all sacred to me for your sweet sake. Ah yes, how truly it is Perfection City, none but I really know."

They walked on again in silence.

"Is there a dog?"

"Yes, but he knows me well. We are coming to the back of the stable now."

"Then go and speak to the dog through the chinks of the logs, else he will bark at me."

Olive crept up quietly, and putting her lips to a crevice in the rough log-stable said softly, "Pluto, good dog!" Pluto answered with a whine of satisfaction, and a soft, purring trumpet from Queen Katharine announced that she too was within, and that she recognised her mistress's voice.

"The horses are here," whispered Olive. "I will go round and bring out Queen Katharine; there is only a wooden bolt on the outside to fasten the door. You had better not go near them for fear of exciting them, which might make the dog bark."

"It is dangerous for you in the dark. I fear the horses may hurt you," said Cotterell, slow in bringing himself to give up the little hand he had held all during that strange night walk.

"I am not afraid of the horses: they know me and I know them," said Olive.

Cotterell heard her talking softly to Queen Katharine as she quietly undid her halter and brought her out of the stable. Not a creature seemed awake in the house, and not a word was spoken by the two as they stole past down to the bars. Once out of earshot, Cotterell sprang upon Queen Katharine and stooping down lifted Olive up before him. She never could quite remember the wild things he said as he rode back to their house, holding her in his arms on the horse. She was dizzy, frightened, and confused, so perhaps he did not say all those wild words, and perhaps she dreamed them. He got Ezra's saddle and put it on Queen Katharine, Olive did not forget to give him the parcel of food and a flask of milk and water, and then he said good-bye. Such a strange good-bye. He knelt before her, clasped her two hands in his own, and said: "Now I know why men have worshipped the image of pure womanhood. It made them better. I shall be made a better man by my worship." And then he was gone without another word, and Olive crept into the house just as the first grey streaks of dawn appeared.

## CHAPTER XVII.

### A LIFE AT STAKE.

WHEN Brother Wright early next morning discovered the loss of the brown mare, he was thrown into a state of the most unphilosophic rage. He had not a moment's doubt as to what had happened, nor a moment's hesitation as to the course he should pursue. He hurried back to the house and without any effort at concealment got out his revolver and stuck it into his belt.

"Wright," said Mary, his wife, "whatever have you got there?" She was filled with amazement.

"A pistol," replied he with firmness.

"What are you going to do with it?"

"Shoot a damned horse-thief, who has been and broken into the stable and stolen Queen Katharine."

He jammed down his hat on his head and made for the door, while Mary Winkle gave a scream that would have done credit to the finest lady in the land.

"You shan't do any such thing! You will be killed! What do you know about pistols? You will be shot by those murderous horse-thieves, and what will become of me—and Willette?" Mary Winkle urged the very arguments that have before now been known to make brave men falter and turn back from running risks.

"I—I shan't do anything rash," said Wright sheepishly. "I'll just go round and rouse the neighbours and see if we can't catch him, he can't have got very far as yet. What beats me is why Pluto didn't bark. The dog's a fool, I'll drown him."

"Oh, I am thankful he didn't bark, for you might have been dead by now if he had. You shan't drown him, for he has saved your life. Horse-thieves are desperate men and wouldn't respect our principles of non-resistance," said Mary Winkle.

"Ahem," said her husband, tucking the revolver out of sight until required.

"What we've got to do is to go to Madame and summon an Assembly of Urgency and talk this matter over, and see what the Community is to do. Wright, you can't go and rouse the neighbours till you've got the sanction of the Assembly. You know that is the rule in all important matters, and this is about the most important matter that has ever come up for discussion."

"Damn discussion!" said Wright angrily. "While we're discussing that thief will get away. Sharp is the word for catching horse-thieves."

"But sharp is not the word for determining the action of Perfection City in an important juncture like the present. Wright, I am surprised at you, and also at your language," said his wife severely.

"Oh these infernal horse-thieves would provoke a saint,—not that I am one," said Wright, still in a rage most unbecoming to a professed non-resistant, and Mary Winkle looked a whole essay full of rebuke at him. She carried the day, however, and together they carried their complaint to Madame.

They found Madame sitting at breakfast along with Uncle David, and being waited upon by a negro-servant, Lucinda, the mother of Napoleon Pompey. The heat of a cooking-stove made Madame ill, therefore she required a servant, and she had what she required, principles of equality to the contrary notwithstanding.

"Dear, dear!" exclaimed Uncle David in much excitement and perturbation. "Wal, to think now o' what big raskills there is in the worl', an' we a-settin' 'em such a good 'xample here o' honesty an' uprightness."

"We must summon the Assembly," said Mary Winkle firmly. "It is a great pity Brothers Ezra and Dummy are both away, but there are quite enough left to deliberate."

"If you think that is the best plan, we had better do it at once, there should be no time wasted," said Madame, looking interrogatively at Brother Wright's frowning face.

"If you ask me——" he began when his wife interrupted him.

"We don't ask you, Wright, at least not until the Assembly of Urgency is convened. Your vote doesn't count for more than mine, and I demand an Assembly."

Wright shrugged his shoulders, and Madame smiled a little sarcastically. "We will summon it," she said.

"An' I'll jes' step roun' an' fetch Sister Olive," said Uncle David, putting on his hat as he spoke, "an' you can bring together the rest of the brethren."

They came quickly enough when they heard of the loss of the brown mare, only Olive was absent. She was ill in bed with a headache and spoke to Uncle David out of a darkened room.

Brother Wright detailed the loss of the horse, while the Assembly listened in deepest attention.

"What we have to consider is the best means of recovering the horse if possible," said Madame. "Does anyone know what is usually done under similar circumstances?"

"The neighbours join together and run down the thief as quickly as possible," said Brother Wright, with sharp emphasis.

"And having run him down, hang him," added Mary Winkle.

"That course is impossible for us," observed Madame.

"That is a point I should like to debate," said Brother Wright. "If we are to live here we must have horses, and we can't keep horses if it is known to be against our principles to shoot a horse-thief. That is all I've got to say."

"An' I want to notice the p'int o' Injuns," said Aunt Ruby. "Ef there's Injuns as will do any wickedness un'er the sun, I want to know are we to sit still an' be roasted on our own fires by wile savages like that, or will the menfolks defen' us as other men do? An' I likewise would wish to p'int out to the 'Sembly as border ruffians is mos'ly as bad as Injuns, an' it stan's to reason as horse-thieves is 'bout the same."

"It seems to me," said Brother Green, speaking with great deliberation, "that our principles were formed and adopted because we thought them right. I don't see in what we should differ from anybody else if we took to the usual prairie arms the moment we felt the shoe pinch! If non-resistance is right, it should be practised against horse-thieves; if it is wrong, then we should be prepared to shoot the thieves of other men's horses. There is no middle course. The throwing away of our settled convictions just because our horse has been stolen is not consistent."

"I'll vote for non-resistance and the maintenance of our principles," said Mary Winkle severely, "and I further think that what is decided by the majority in this meeting should bind all the members."

She fixed her eye upon Wright with meaning.

"It is a most difficult juncture," remarked Madame. "I wish much we had the help of Brother Ezra's wisdom to guide us."

"Yes," said Uncle David cordially, "an' sister Olive too."

"I do not see how Sister Olive can have any experience that would enable her to give good advice on this subject," said Madame acidly.

"Oh, Sister Olive has consider'ble 'cuteness," remarked Uncle David. "Now you'd be 'stonished to hear the wise things she says, an' she as purty as a kitten or a rose all the while."

"Then I guess we'll just do nothing at all? Is that the decision of this Assembly?" asked Brother Wright abruptly.

"There is great force in passive resistance," said Brother Carpenter, a boneless individual who counted for little either for work in the fields, or for advice in the councils, of Perfection City. "Where passive resistance has been applied by large numbers and for a long time it has effected great changes," he observed conversationally.

"I think principles are principles," said Brother Green, "and may not be lightly set aside."

"Well, I guess I'll go home then, since nothing is going to be done," said Brother Wright angrily, "and I'll try and keep hold of the last horse, else that thief will come and take him too, when he finds what fools he's got to deal with."

The Assembly broke up, having decided nothing at all, and having only succeeded in embittering the feelings of several persons, and in widening the chasm of differences which had revealed itself in the course of the debate, a result that has often followed the meeting of larger and more notorious Assemblies.

Although Brother Wright could not now violate one of the fundamental doctrines of Perfection City, it was open to him to use a little worldly wisdom in the way of setting others upon the track of the thief. Accordingly, without saying a single word to Mary Winkle or anyone else, he mounted Rebel and proceeded to rouse the neighbours who were not at all bound by non-resistant theories. Nothing gets up a prairie man's anger quicker than the knowledge that a horse-thief has begun active operations in his vicinity. Horses are absolutely necessary to his daily life, and to be suddenly deprived of his horses is one of the greatest calamities that can overtake a settler. They can take a merciful view of homicide at times, but never of horse-stealing. Brother Wright relied on this known propensity, and by visiting the most hardy of his neighbours had before night started as relentless a set of hunters after Queen Katharine as ever put leg over horse or drew pistol from belt.

Olive meanwhile remained at home all unconscious

of what had taken place at the Assembly, and of the pursuit organized afterwards as the effect of Brother Wright's embassies. She had decided in her own mind that the best course for her to adopt was to keep absolute silence until Ezra should come home. To him she would explain everything, and she felt convinced that he was just enough, albeit no friend of Cotterell's, to be ready to sacrifice a horse in order to facilitate his escape. She did not feel at all so sure about some of the other members of the Community. At all events Cotterell's best chance of safety lay in her keeping firmly to her resolution of silence about him. The best way for her to keep silent without exciting suspicion was not to talk with anyone, and feeling pretty well convinced that somebody would come to talk over the great calamity with her, she resolved to be out of the way. In any case she was very miserable and very anxious, and could not stay at home, so she wandered off for a walk. She went to the spring, then she went to Weddell's Gully and looked at the black burnt waste. She tried to think about the interest and excitement of the fire, but could think of nothing but Cotterell riding for his life and of the men who were riding after him. Olive knew nothing of the second set of men sent after the horse-thief; her mind was still anxiously dwelling on the probability of his being captured by those who had " wanted " him for the murder of Jake Mills. The fact was, however, that this first hunting-party had given over their quest, for a man must be caught by the second day on the prairie if he is to be caught at all. This, however, Olive did not know, and she kept wondering and picturing all sorts of terrible possibilities. Had the men found the trail? Would Queen Katharine hold out till he got to the border? True she had been resting for a whole day, but then a man's life depended on her endurance, and Olive remembered with a cold dread that Queen Katharine was only a farm-horse and not trained to such desperate efforts as this. Then she remembered the others, those dreadful hunters, were also mounted on farm-horses, and this thought gave her some small comfort. She came home again after a most wretched day spent in aimless rambling over the hopeless black prairie and crept up to the out-side platform to scan once more that dreary waste towards the endless western horizon. Far away towards the north-west she saw a band of horsemen huddled together and moving rapidly in an easterly direction. Olive's heart stood still with terror. Oh! who were they? And why were they riding rapidly? Men rode in bands to funerals, but then they went slowly: they rode fast only when out on a man-hunt. She did not call up Napoleon Pompey, although he could see like a hawk; she dreaded to hear what his explanation would be. She watched with straining eyes until the men had disappeared within the belt of timber that marked the course of the Creek, then she came downstairs with her miserable discovery hidden in her heart.

The next day dragged slowly by, Olive feeling more and more wretched and anxious each moment, and longing for Ezra's return. Napoleon Pompey did nothing but speculate about the horse-thief and the probabilities of his capture. He regaled Olive with accounts of the numbers of men out on the hunt, the desperate character of their courage, and the murderous accuracy of their aim with revolvers. Sick at heart she had to listen to him and try and collect her terrified senses in order to make occasional comments and replies. Again she hid herself away from her neighbours and spent most of the day in a corn-stack, not two hundred yards from the house, whence she could see plainly without being seen. Uncle David came and stayed so long waiting for her, that she nearly smothered in the corn-stack before he went away, and she was able to come out and catch a breath of fresh air. Then Aunt Ruby came and peered all about everywhere, even down into the cellar, and stayed a good while there examining Olive's milk-pans, until Olive bethought herself of the device of sending off Diana to hasten Aunt Ruby's exit from the cellar. This device succeeded: Aunt Ruby was so dismayed at seeing that redoubable puppy lolluping up to her that she incontinently fled, and Olive emerged once more from the suffocation of the corn-stack.

Mary Winkle came twice, fortunately without Willette, for that astute young person would instantly have discovered Olive, owing to the pertinacious company of Diana. A dog does not hang around a cornstack the live-long day unless there is something interesting inside it claiming attention. Olive began to feel like a hunted criminal herself.

Napoleon Pompey had been sent away in the morning to look for some young cattle that had not been seen since the fire, and having to go on foot he did not come back till the afternoon. He burst in upon her with these appalling words:

"Dey's done cotch him!"

"Who told you?" asked Olive, not pretending any miscomprehension of what was only too plain to her mind.

"Ole nigger seed 'em. Dey bringin' him back. Ole man Cotterell he de hoss-thief, him ridin' Queen Katharine when dey cotch him. Nigger tole me he seed 'em yonder."

"Have they shot him?" asked Olive with white lips.

"No, dey's gwine ter jury-try him, den dey hang him 'cause he done stole hoss and he kill ole Mill's Jake." Napoleon Pompey licked his lips and grinned. Olive turned from him in horror.

"Where have they taken him to?"

"Dunno. Nigger he 'lowed dey gwine ter Jacksonville."

Olive made up her mind and took her resolution. She questioned Napoleon Pompey very carefully, found exactly what negro it was from whom he had obtained his information concerning the capture of Cotterell. He worked with the Halls who lived over the other side of Cotton Wood Creek, and she made minute inquiries as to how to reach their house. Then she told the boy to give Rebel a double feed of corn and to bring in the new lariat-rope and mallet and pin. Rebel had been removed back to his own stable by Brother Wright's desire, as he had no belief now in Pluto as a watch-dog. Napoleon Pompey was open-mouthed with wonder at Olive's directions about the horse, and asked "whar she gwine?" She told him to do as she bid him and to say nothing to anybody about it, whereat he was still more open-mouthed. Olive got a large shawl and rolled it up into a tight bundle, and then dressed herself in a strong serviceable stuff dress and went to supper with Napoleon Pompey, to whom she never spoke a single word. When supper was over she sent him down to his mother to ask her to bake a pumpkin-pie for her. Napoleon Pompey said he would go "fust thing in de mornin'," and she told him sternly to go at once and do as he was bid. When Napoleon Pompey came back Olive was gone, and so was Rebel, with lariat-rope picket-pin and mallet, and so was her tightly rolled shawl.

Perfection City had further cause for amazement and hurried meeting in Assembly.

Olive, meanwhile, was riding fast towards Cotton Wood Creek which she reached and crossed by the last shreds of daylight. She stumbled up out of the bottom-lands on to the high prairie, then perceiving by the sound of Rebel's hoofs that at last she had struck grass again, for the fire had not crossed the Creek, she determined to camp. It was a black night, but she knew how to drive her picket and unsaddle her horse blindfold. Taking her saddle and shawl out of the circle of Rebel's night-range, she wrapped herself up to wait until daylight should permit her again to go forward. She was not in the least frightened, although the prairie wolves were yelping in the distance. The nervous terrors that had beset her when sitting in her own comfortable little kitchen with her dog at her feet, and a stout lad in the room overhead, were quite gone. Yet there was enough to frighten a more valiant person than our poor little Olive, with her half-defined thoughts and her generous impulses.

What was it she proposed to herself in this expedition? First of all to overtake Cotterell and his captors, and then to do what the wit of woman could devise to save him from their fury. In her ignorance of prairie feelings and ideas she attached no importance to the fact that he would have been captured riding the well-known brown mare belonging to Perfection City. He would of course explain that she had lent him the animal, and that question would at once drop out of the debate. Then the terrible one of the shooting of Jake Mills would have to be settled. That was what she feared for Cotterell, and that was where her testimony and pleading might avail. She knew from his own lips how the fatal affray had occurred, and she would be able in some measure, perhaps, to counteract the evidence of that wicked lying negro who out of revenge was going to swear away Cotterell's life. Olive hated to do it, but she knew she could say things to any western jury that would make it difficult for them to admit negro evidence. For once in a way the mighty race-prejudice could be relied upon to work for justice, and poor Olive, fanatical friend of the negro, had to confess she was glad to have so strong a lever to her hand in this dreadful emergency.

Meanwhile the never-ending night wore on. How long, how unutterably long are the hours of darkness to them who wait sleeplessly for the dawn! The twinkling stars passed over her head, and Olive tried to fix her eyes steadily on one or two of them in order to convince herself that they really did move after all. Thus staring at the stars, her eyes became weary, and the lids dropped slowly over them, and she fell into a troubled sleep, haunted with fearsome visions.

She must have slept some little time, for when she awoke the stars had certainly changed places and were moreover becoming pale in the first grey streaks of morning. Olive awoke shivering with cold and drenched with the heavy prairie dew. Her teeth chattered, so she could hear them like a piece of broken machinery moving inside her head, while her fingers were almost numb. As soon as she could make out Rebel in the approaching dawn, she saddled him, and, woman-like, did not forget the lariat-rope, picket-pin and mallet, even in the midst of her terrible anxiety. She thought of Cotterell in the hands of his foes, and the recollection came back to her, like a blow that almost stunned her, that this would be the last time he would ever see the sun rise unless she hurried to his rescue. The thought spurred her to renewed activity, the horror of it drove the chilled blood with a rush to her heart. She caught her breath, and then felt hot. She did not shiver any more, and her chattering teeth were set in a desperate resolve. She clambered up on the horse's back and set off at a gallop towards that house where she would get positive news which would help her to find the lynching-party quickly. Ah! merciful God! The lynching-party! She urged Rebel into a harder gallop, for the sun was just beginning to appear over the horizon, and she could see where she was going. She reached the cabin where the Halls lived in due course. They didn't know her, but they invited her to breakfast with prairie courtesy. She saw the negro man who had told the news to Napoleon Pompey.

"Yes, he seed 'em totin' ole man Cotterell back." There was never any doubt in Olive's mind as to the fact that they had caught him, what she wanted to know was the destination of the party. "He 'lowed dey was gwine ter Jacksonville, 'cause down yonder was whar dey hang de las' man; den dey jury-try him, an' Jacksonville mighty handy anyhow, dar heaps o' trees dar."

Olive could not repress a shudder of horror which the negro saw, and so did the Halls. She would not stop a moment to eat a bit of breakfast, notwithstanding their urgent entreaties, but got directions as to the shortest road to Jacksonville and hastened away on her errand of mercy.

Mrs. Hall looking after her rapidly vanishing figure, and remembering the look of misery on her face, "reckoned 'twas one o' them po' silly gals as is cotched by a yaller 'stache. She was powerful sorry for her anyhow, she 'peared mos' broke down an' sick. She 'lowed if the boys hed hung ole man Cotterell when Glover's gal shot herself 'cause he wouldn't marry her, 'twould hev been a sight better anyhow." Her husband was of opinion that "gals was fules gapin' a'ter strangers an' furrin fellers, not bein' content along o' their nat'ral men-folks as b'longed to 'em, app'inted by the hand o' Providence."

Olive rode through the hot September day feeling very faint and tired, but never for a moment faltering in her determination; and well on in the afternoon she came to Jacksonville, a place with two houses standing and the stakes for three more stuck into the ground to signify possession. There was only one woman in the place along with a flock of children. No sign of men anywhere. The woman did not know much about the movements of the "boys." "They hadn't passed that way at all, but she hearn tell they had been out catching a horse-thief and murderer, and they had caught him too, a Britisher, she was told, and it was a shame those foreigners should be allowed to come to America to steal honest folks horses, and true born Americans too, as always worked for every cent before they spent it. They had taken him to Union Mills to try him and she hoped—well she didn't want to say anything unbecoming to a professing Christian, but wouldn't Olive come in and eat a bit and rest before going further, she didn't look fit for such hard riding." Olive, feeling sick with disappointment, accepted a morsel of food, and asking her way to Union Mills started off. She had come thirty-eight miles already, and if she had only known where to go she would have been there hours ago. It was nearly twenty miles to Union Mills, she could not hope to reach it that night, but she started nevertheless although the sun was getting low in the west. The horrid thought kept pressing against her heart: was she already too late? But no, she would force it out of her mind, and come what might she would never stop until she had done her utmost to save him. She therefore pressed forward, but Rebel showed signs of giving out. He lay down with her suddenly and tried to roll. This would never do. All depended on her horse, if he failed her then Cotterell's last chance of life was gone. She rode slowly, now following a prairie track and now riding along side it, because Rebel stumbled in the ruts. It got dark, she did not know where she was, but followed the track for some time mechanically. A light suddenly showed up on her left. Rebel pricked up his ears and turned towards it. After some difficulty she reached the door. Could they harbour her for the night? She was caught out and could go no further.

"Land o' Goshen! 'course they could, an' whar in sin was she gwine that time o' night 'thout nobody, not even a dawg?" Olive said it was a case of life and death and she must do it. They were deeply sorry, they fed her with corn-bread and bacon, they fed her horse, and were kindness itself. The cabin had only one room with a bed in one corner for the man and his wife. Olive was desperately tired. The wife said "she'd be doggauned sick 'less she went to bed." So Olive lay down on the bed, and the settler's wife lay down beside her, and the man slept on the floor with his head on a pile of corn-shucks. Long before daylight he went out and fed her horse. The wife cooked a good breakfast and pressed Olive again and again "to scrouge down suthin' more," and sent her off with many good wishes as to her finding her husband better, who, she was sure, 'ud be tickled to death at seeing her.

## CHAPTER XVIII.

#### LYNCH LAW.

UNION MILLS was full of people, mostly men, and Phillipps' Store, which was the only shop in the place, as well as being the Post-Office, was crowded to suffocation. Those who couldn't get inside stood around the door talking loudly as they chewed their tobacco. Inside the talking and tobacco-chewing were carried on likewise. A ring of men were sitting on barrels and nail-kegs and coils of rope and extemporized chairs of all kinds. Of these, twelve arranged together at one side formed the jury, and the rest were witnesses and spectators. In their midst stood Cotterell. He was not bound or specially guarded in any way, but he was unarmed, while pistols hung at the belts of all the other men there. Cotterell held his head erect, his eyes looked clear, and his lips were firm. A careful observer might have noticed that his nostrils sometimes twitched, but his hands were perfectly steady. Yet he was on trial for his life, without appeal and without a friend in "the court." Several of the men had asked him questions which he had answered, shortly and sharply perhaps, but with a perfectly steady voice.

"I dunno what we're gwine on talkin' for," said a jury man with a twang that bespoke Arkansas. "Hain't it clar this hyar feller, what was wanted for the shootin' o' Ole Mills' boy, he's the same cuss as stole the mare from them damned fools up to 'Fection City? He's got ter be hanged, anyhow. I want ter go home. I hain't a-gwine to stick hyar all day, by Gosh!"

"I did not steal the mare," said Cotterell, his nostrils dilating.

"You hear that," said the foreman, who sat on a sugar-barrel.

"You was ridin' her when we come up t'yer," said one who had been out on the hunt.

"I was."

"How 'd yer git her then 'cept by stealin'?"

"She was lent to me by one of the members of the Community," said Cotterell.

"They's damn fools, I know, but I reckon they hain't such all-fired damn fools as ter give their best hoss ter you," said the man from Arkansas.

Cotterell's lips curled with contempt, but he did not speak.

"Look hyar, fellow jurymen," said one of them who prided himself on the accuracy of his language on all occasions. "I'd axe leave ter make a few remarks. We were informed by the gentlemen what caught the prisoner that they were notified o' the stealing by one o' them Perfection City fellers. If the horse was lent how is it the owner didn't know about the lending?"

"Yes," said one of the gentlemen referred to, "ole man Wright, he come and tol' me 'bout the stealin' o' the hoss, an' he 'lowed, on'y it was agin his principles, he'd like ter hev been out with the boys. It don't 'pear ter my min' as there was much len'ing 'bout it."

"'This trial, gen'lemen, is all fair and square an' 'cordin' to law. We'll settle this p'int 'fore we go further," said the foreman. "You say the horse was lent to you?"

"I do say so emphatically," replied the prisoner.

"Wal, we've got one o' them 'Fection City fellers to say the hoss was stolen, he'll swear to that, an' I reckon by their idees he was part-owner of it anyhow. Now, that's the witness agin yer. Who have you got to swear yer was lent the horse fair and square?"

"I have had no chance of getting any witness, as you very well know," replied Cotterell.

"Wal, I reckon yo' hev bin kep' purty toler'ble close. Anyhow, it shan't be said as we hain't gi'en yer a good chance. Now, which might be yer witness to the len'ing? There hain't such a damn sight o' folks up to 'Fection City as 'ud make yer forget so ready as all that."

Cotterell hesitated.

"Hain't yo' got no tongue? Who lent yer the hoss, I say?" repeated the foreman.

"Mrs. Weston," said Cotterell at last.

"That's a lie, anyhow," burst out one of the bystanders.

"It is not a lie, it is the truth," said Cotterell hotly.

"Wal, now, see hyar. I was over to ole man Weston's, an' I seed Mis' Weston myself, an' she tole me she hadn't sot eyes on yer. Now then?"

It was Owen who spoke, he had been out, as we know, on the first hunting-party and was now present as a spectator. He would have been on the jury, only it was considered more delicate for him to stand aside, considering that he had been out to catch Cotterell, and prairie men are punctilious in the observance of all those forms of etiquette with which they are familiar. Although not on the jury, Owen was quite free to intervene in the trial, he was one of the foremost settlers on the prairie. Cotterell looked hard at him as he spoke.

"Did she tell you that herself?" he asked, drawing his eye-brows tightly together.

"Yes, she tole me herself," replied Owen.

"Then I have nothing further to say," said Cotterell, setting his teeth grimly under his moustache. He realised very clearly what he was doing, he was throwing away his last chance of life; but his resolution never wavered for a moment. The thought flashed through his mind that most people would think him a fool to act as he did, risk the certainty of death for the sake of a fantastic loyalty to a woman who could never be to him anything but the distant friend another man's wife should be. Then came the recollection that no one, not even she for whom he was sacrificing his life, would ever know what he had done. There was something fantastic surely in all this. Their whole acquaintance had been fantastic in a sense: Mr. Perseus was a fancy, but how dangerously sweet it had been while it lasted. And now it was over, he would never hear the sound of her voice again nor feel the touch of her little hand. Poor child! He could well imagine, with that jealous husband of hers, how she might have been driven to save herself from his anger by declaring she had never seen him. Jealousy was a monster surely, if there ever was a monster on this earth. Cotterell almost smiled to himself as he thought how once again he would act the part of Perseus to the unhappy one and save her by his silence from the monster's fangs. Thoughts such as these swept through his mind as he stood facing the jury, while they were somewhat nonplussed as to their future proceedings owing to his determination not to say anything further. It appeared almost indecent to hang a man who would not argue out the points with them: they had never met such a one before.

"There's a gal hyar a-wantin' ter come in," said

one of the men who was standing just outside the door.

"Keep her hout," said one of the jury. "We hain't agoin' ter hev any women a screech-owlin' hyar. It's one o' his gals as he's lef' to die maybe of a broken heart 'thout the satisfaction o' bein' a widder."

"Let me pass, please," said an imperious little voice that thrilled Cotterell to the heart. "I am one of the witnesses in this trial. I have important evidence to give."

The men fell back and left the passage free. Western men, even armed ones, can't do anything against a woman.

Olive came into the crowded room, Olive dirty, dishevelled, travel-stained, her face begrimed with prairie dust, her hair unkempt, her dress crumpled and with many a rent in it. Cotterell hardly knew her.

"Who mought yer be, miss?" inquired one of the jury.

"I am Mrs. Weston."

"Whar's yer husband? Yer hadn't oughter be hyar a follerin' this feller roun' the prairie. Tain't——"

"Shut yer mouth or I'll send a bullet down yer gullet," roared the foreman, putting his hand to his revolver. "Take a cheer," he added, gallantly offering Olive the sugar-barrel upon which he had been sitting in his official capacity.

"No, thank you," said Olive. "I will stand."

She took her place beside Cotterell, but without looking at him or addressing a single word to him.

"What are you trying this man for?" she asked, facing the jury dauntlessly.

"Wal, mos'ly fur stealin' yer hoss," said one of them.

"He didn't steal it. I myself lent him the horse. It belongs to us," was the reply.

"By Gosh!" exclaimed Owen, "you tole me yerself yer hadn't sot n'ary an eye on him."

"So I hadn't when you were there, he did not come until the next day."

The jury whistled collectively and incredulously.

"Silence!" said the foreman.

"I can now explain," said Cotterell. "I didn't go to Mrs. Weston's house until two days after—after Mills' death——"

"A'ter yer killed him," corrected Owen.

"And you were there the next day," concluded Cotterell, not taking any notice of the interruption.

"Yes, that is it. Mr. Cotterell came the next evening but one after the prairie fire, and I gave him the mare to go away on, because his colt broke loose from the bars in the dark." Olive spoke quite quietly, with no trace of excitement beyond a knitting of her pretty eye-brows.

"Wal, I reckon we hain't got nuthin' more to do then," said one of the jury-men, getting up from his nail-keg and strapping up his holster.

"There's the murder too," objected one, "not as I put it fust noways, on'y we might go inter it now, seein' there hain't nuthin' ter be got outer the hoss-stealin' business."

"Yer hain't got evidence for the murder case too, has yer?" sneered the man who had been so peremptorily silenced by the foreman on his first objection to Olive's presence.

"Only this. You are not non-resistants, are you?"

"We hain't such blasted fools," observed the Arkansas man genially.

"Well, then, when this poor Jake Mills in his drunken fury came up and fired at Mr. Cotterell, was he or was he not to fire in self-defence, according to your ideas and practice?"

"Of course he was," said the jury in unison.

"Then that is what he did. Jake Mills fired first."

"Two shots," said Cotterell in a low voice, but every man in the room heard him distinctly.

"That coloured man we saw yesterday swore that Cotterell lay in wait for Mills, and fired from under cover as he came up to the house," said a man from Illinois who had not spoken hitherto.

"Wal now," said the Arkansas man, "I didn't say nuthin' 'bout that yesterday. Long as it was hoss-stealin' we knowed whar we was an' what we hed ter do, 'cause we hed the hoss. But this hyar shootin' business hain't noways the same. Any gen'leman hyar might hev a difference with any other gen'leman, an' 's long as it were done fair, I don't see as how anyone hes any business to say they shouldn't settle it with pistols or bowie-knives accordin' to taste. We are all for freedom in this country I reckon, an' that's how it hes been done in Arkansas often an' satisfact'ry."

"This ain't Arkansas, an' we are determined to put a stop to this shootin' round everyday," said the Illinois man firmly. "It ain't respectable and it stops quiet settlers from coming here to take farms. We are going to stop it."

"Then you should have stopped Jake Mills when he went to Mr. Cotterell's and fired at him first," said Olive quickly.

"There's somethin' in that," said the foreman, whose native gallantry led him to side with a pretty woman. "In a trial we hev to consider all the p'ints o' the case. I consider that as for the horse-stealin', that hes mostly broke down under evidence. We must now go into the other charge, which is shootin' Jake Mills, an' a damned scoundrel he was too."

The jury laughed pleasantly at this sally from the bench, or to speak more accurately from the sugar-barrel. Even Cotterell seemed a trifle amused, only Olive did not unknit her eyebrows, nor did the hard lines around her mouth in the least relax.

"We are in consider'ble difficulty 'bout this here shootin' case," continued the foreman when the mirth had subsided, "and if I had knowed as that was all we was up for tryin', I don't reckon we 'ud all on us ha' been here as is now collected together to maintain the rights an' freedom o' our country."

The jury murmured applause, upon recognising well-known Fourth of July phrases, which have perennial power to stir the American breast.

"Why ain't we agoin' on with this blamed trial?" asked an impatient jury-man. "We hev purty nigh lost a whole day's work a'ready an' hain't finished nothin' yit. When we strung up ole Howard for hoss-stealin' we hed the job done clar up afore noon, an' we could go home to dinner comfor'ble."

Olive gave a faint inarticulate cry and put her hands up to her ears, or was it perchance to her neck? Cotterell turned anxiously towards her as if she was going to faint, and he would catch her before she fell. She steadied herself in an instant and again faced the jury like a tiny lioness, small in body but with unconquerable courage.

"Well, gen'lemen, I'm agreeable to proceed with the evidence," said the foreman graciously.

"I was told we had evidence o' deliberate murder," said the Illinois juror.

"We most on us hearn what the nigger said," remarked another carelessly, "some on us fooled roun' with that yesterday an' lost a fair half day's work."

"Wal, gen'lemen, you could ha' had the nigger again here to-day, on'y it was not considered necessary, as we was mostly of opinion to fin' a true bill on the horse-stealin' count. We can sen' for the nigger. He's mos' likely sneakin' roun' here. Them niggers is jes' like buzzards, they can scent out where there's a hangin',—ahem, gen'lemen, we'll proceed," said the foreman, suddenly recollecting himself and Olive's presence barely in time.

"I vote for sending for the coloured man," said the Illinois juror firmly. "We'll confront him with the prisoner."

"Nigger be damned!" roared the Arkansas man jumping violently off his nail-keg. "Yo' reckon I'm agoin' ter sit hyar an' see a white man hanged on nigger evidence. No, sir. I won't stan' such a insult to my race as that. There be some things a man o' honour won't stan' an' that's one o' them. Thar hain't no man spryer to light out an' catch a hoss-thief nor I be, an' I'll do my dooty in the hangin' too, an' hol' the rope as tight as ony o' yo'all. But I'll bust up afore I'll take nigger evidence 'gin a white man. I reckon there hain't none o' yo' gen'lemen as is pertikler sot on that nigger, be yer?"

Olive's heart gave a bound of joy as the Arkansas juror poured forth his torrent of protest. Alas, poor Olive and her high-flown love of the black race! She was bound to confess that her best hope for effecting the end she was struggling for, lay in the blind race-prejudice of this ignorant Southerner.

"I guess we ought to take all the evidence, white

or black, that bears on the case," observed he of Illinois.

"If that thar nigger comes inter this hyar room to conten' with this hyar jury an' give his evidence, I'll shoot him, 'fore he gits over that door-sill, so I will, by God, an' no man as knows me ever said I went back o' my word in shootin'."

The Arkansas juror faced them with his black eyes ablaze and his dark visage twitching with suppressed fury. He was quivering under the sting of what was to him an intolerable insult, and there was nothing he would not do to wipe out that insult.

Olive looked at Cotterell for the first time, and as their eyes met he was horrified to see the white, drawn expression on her face. He attributed it to the very natural womanly fear that she might be involved in a promiscuous shooting affray in that crowded room.

"Don't be alarmed, they will not bring the negro in here," he said soothingly.

"I am not afraid for myself," she answered, simply and truthfully.

"Wal, gen'lemen," said the foreman pleasantly. "I reckon we hev finished for this spell anyhow. I consider the prisoner hes hed as fair a trial as ony man could wish, and I hev on'y ter thank yer all for yer help upon this occasion in maintain' the laws and freedom of our beloved country, as belongs to the duty of free-born citizens."

"Hurrah!" said the jury, with another relapse into Fourth of Julyism.

"We've purty nigh lost two whole days' work 'long o' this hyar foolin'," observed the Arkansas man angrily. "Them coons up to 'Fection City is nat'ral born fools anyhow. Fust they blaze roun' an' set us on ter run down a hoss-thief fur 'em. Soon as we've done cotch him, they sen' roun' a woman to say the hoss was lent. If the blamed critters come to me again, reckon I'll stick to my plough-handles. I'll not light out for them, you bet." And he immediately walked out of the store followed by the entire jury and the foreman.

When the Court broke up, Olive and Cotterell were left alone in the store along with Phillipps, the storekeeper. The latter handed Cotterell his revolver, which the jury had considerately left for him.

"I suppose I'm a free man," said Cotterell, with more sign of emotion in his manner than he had yet shown.

"Thanks to Mrs. Weston you are free," said Phillipps.

He turned to Olive, who seemed in a daze, and said, "Shall we go now?"

"Yes," she answered, and they left the store together.

The crowd in the road before the door was already fast dispersing. The exciting climax for which they had waited was not to come off, so there remained no further inducement to stay. Some straggled into the smithy, some went towards the mills, but most of the men were getting their horses, putting on saddles, and settling halters and reins. The Arkansas man had a waggon and was hitching his horses to it, as Olive, riding on Rebel, and Cotterell on Queen Katharine, passed by.

"Be yo' gwine with him?" asked the Arkansas man, pointing to Olive.

"Yes," said Olive shortly.

"Wish we'd hanged the damned cuss 'fore she come in," said the Arkansas man regretfully to his companion, who had also been present at the trial. "She's gwine ter 'lope with him, an' ole man Weston he on'y jes' married her las' spring."

"Reckon she don't like 'Fection City idees. Gals mos' allers likes a fightin' man best, an' this hyar one is reg'lar downright handsome too."

"If we'd on'y hed a-hanged him she couldn't hev run off with the coon," repeated the Arkansas man with conviction, shaking his head sorrowfully as he watched the two disappearing among the trees on the South Fork.

## CHAPTER XIX.

### OLIVE MISSING.

THERE was dire dismay at Perfection City when the flight of Olive became known. Napoleon Pompey informed Madame of it the same evening, but, for reasons best known to herself, she did not announce the fact until the next morning, when the brethren and sisters flocked to her house to talk over this surprising event in all its bearings. The members accounted for it in different ways and explained it according to their preconceived notions. Madame at once said that she had evidently left her husband whom she had never really loved at all.

"I think we must all have noticed how utterly unsuited she was to him and how uncongenial. She was no fit companion for a man of Ezra's mind," said Madame.

"Wal, now," observed Uncle David, "I think such a purty little gal with sweet little kitten-ways was a most congenial companion."

"Uncle, you don't understand men. Men with minds and high aspirations want a companion capable of sharing their ideas and aims, they don't want a kitten or a plaything."

"My 'pinion is most men is satisfied with kittens, if they're as soft an' coaxin' in their ways as little Ollie is," replied Uncle David.

"I guess she couldn't stand the bondage of marriage," said Mary Winkle. "When she first came she was all for being absorbed in her husband, she would be Mrs. Weston forsooth, she wanted to sink her individuality. She has naturally found out her mistake. I respect her and sympathize with her in her efforts to shake off the trammels of custom and make a dash for freedom. I dare say we shall soon have her coming back again, having resumed her own name, and perhaps ready to lecture on the absurdity of women giving up their names on marriage, as if they ceased to exist. Marriage under these circumstances becomes a sort of death to a woman. It is extinction."

"'Tain't no such thing, Sister Mary," said Uncle David. "It is an honourable distinction our forefathers have used, findin' the same handy and convenient. I don't believe little Ollie has gone a-lecterin', she ain't that sort o' gal. I guess she's jes' tired an' lonesome feelin', an' thought she'd ride out an' meet Ezry comin' home."

"She hasn't done that, Uncle, for I've seen a man from over Jacksonville way, and he told me she had been seen the other side of Big Cotton Wood Creek, and that she was asking for news of Cotterell," said Brother Wright.

"Then she has gone to him," said Madame with decision.

"She hain't neither," contradicted Uncle David, "you hain't got no business to tell wicked stories like that."

"She has been carrying on a secret acquaintance with him all the summer. I know that, for I surprised them together at the spring some weeks ago."

"She didn't do nothin' that was dishonest an' secret," said Uncle David anxiously. "I ain't a-goin' ter believe anything 'gin little Ollie. She's a good little gal."

He wiped his forehead nervously with his large bony hand, and then took out his red handkerchief and passed it several times across his face.

"The power of love is strong," said Madame, looking at him with compassion.

"Yes, yes," he replied quickly, "jes' what I say, an' she did love her husban', an' hain't done nothin' wrong."

"She didn't love him," burst out Madame with excitement. "It often filled me with anger to see how she took all his love and made no return. Every one saw it."

"I guess the rest of us didn't pay so much attention to them and their affairs. We had our own," said Mary Winkle, at which Madame winced.

"You don't know what her feelin's was. She loved Ezry, else she wouldn't ha' married him an' followed him way out here on this lonesome prairie. I ain't never goin' to believe wrong o' little Ollie." Uncle David's big chest heaved with a sob that would burst out.

Madame placed her hand gently upon his. "The falling of one's idol has always been a grievous sorrow, and has bruised many a loving heart."

"She wasn't fit to live here on the prairie," said Aunt Ruby, wiping her spectacles with her big checked handkerchief. "She was too young an' purty an' frolicksome to be here anyhow. Ezry hed ought ter hev kep' her in the East, where she was raised, an' where she could go to parties, an' put on purty clo's, an' dance, an' so forth. It's nat'ral for them young gals to dance an' love fin'ry, jes' as it's nat'ral for lambs to skip an' play in the sunshine. They is born so, an' I guess the Lord put the right idees into their min's at the beginnin'. I don' wan' ter skip, an' Sister Mary she don't wan' ter neither, we hev got ole an' stiff by now; but that chile she did wan' ter, on'y mos' likely she didn't know it. Sweet purty little thing, too, she was, it done my eyes good ter look at her. She wasn't fit for 'Fection City, we hain't got nothin' for young folks as don't care mos'ly to argy 'bout principles, they loves ter be gay. Why, it wasn't further back nor day 'fore yesterday she come ter my house 'long with that pup o' hern. My stars, didn't she laugh when it took ter scootin' roun' 'mong my hens! It done me a heap o' good ter hear her, it was like a silver bell, an' she hedn't nothin' for to amuse her. I think it was down-right sinful o' Brother Ezry to take such a sweet purty little thing 'way from her proper home."

Aunt Ruby ended her long speech with the twin-sob to the one that had escaped from Uncle David.

"Sister, you're a down-right good woman," said he gratefully. The two old people nodded at each other in complete harmony of affection and affliction.

A long day passed over Perfection City, a day without any positive news or confirmation of previous rumours. The brethren were full of their various theories in regard to Olive's disappearance, which they found necessary to discuss and re-discuss over and over again. All work was at a stand-still, for the members congregated at Madame's house both early and late, as they considered she would be the first to get any news from the outside world. Without a horse they were practically cut off from all communication with the outside, and were entirely dependent on the thoughtfulness of such neighbours as might come to bring them news. It was in the afternoon of the day of the abortive trial at Union Mills that the first authentic tidings reached them. They were talking the matter over together for the fiftieth time when Brother Green was seen coming very hurriedly from his forge along with a stranger, who waited outside the door with an amount of diffidence unusual on the prairie. Brother Green's grimy face wore a look of alarm.

"We've got news of them both," he exclaimed, bursting into the room regardless of ceremony, he who was generally the most heedful of the little forms of politeness. "She has gone after him, and they've gone away, and he stole her and said we lent her to him," said Brother Green distractedly.

"Brother, I don't understand," said Madame. "Who lent what? And where has she gone?"

"I mean Sister Olive—oh! I'm so sorry—poor Brother Ezra!—Sister Olive has gone off with Cotterell, and it was he who stole Queen Katharine, only it was proved at the trial that she lent her to him."

Brother Green was too distressed to be a good witness.

"Who told you?" asked Madame.

"Whoever did told a lie," said Uncle David. "He's outside. He was at the trial and has come to tell us about it."

"Then bring him in," said Madame.

The stranger entered, looking somewhat abashed. He was truly sorry to be the bearer of such bad tidings.

"Young man, before you begin this wicked tale, I charge you think of God and tell the truth." Uncle David stood before him like an avenging spirit.

"Sir, excuse him," said Madame in her sweet voice. "The old man is painfully distracted by grief, he does not know what he is saying. You have come to bring us definite news, have you not?"

"I'm thund'rin' sorry, so I am, an' if we'd ha' knowed how it would ha' ended, the boys 'ud ha' made sure by hangin' him fust an' havin' the trial a'terwards."

"Are you speaking about Mr. Cotterell? We have not had any news for days, so perhaps you will explain it all clearly," said Madame.

"Yes, wal, when ole man Wright come an' tole as how yer hoss was stole, the boys they 'lowed as you was all such damn—such all-fired pertikler folks as didn't do yer own shootin', they 'lowed they oughter kinder be neighbourly an' do it for yer. So we sot out to run down the cuss. We got word from a teamster from beyond the Creek, he seed a man on a mare jes' like yourn agoin' toward the border. So we picked up the trail right away. He warn't worth a red cent to hide a trail. He jes' follered straight ahead 'long the road, axin' his way an' follerin' plumb on the d'rections. Any fool could ha' run down such a coon as him. He war ridin' yer brown mare when they come up, an' he didn't show fight, jes' said he'd stan' trial, an' he 'lowed it 'ud be fair. The boys calkerlated it wouldn't be a fair trial 'less they toted him roun' to Union Mills, which are his own post-office, an' if that ain't treatin' a man fair nothin' is. An' they got a new set o' men to stan' jury as what cotch him, 'cause mos' on 'em was that mad for leavin' the corn-shuckin' to run down such a nat'ral-born fool, they'd ha' mos' likely strung him slap up. It war all done fair, we kep' him down to Phillipps' store over night, an' I tuk a spell o' stan'in' guard. We didn't sen' for none o' yo'uns, 'cause we knowed yer be all sot agin hangin', an' yer can't have a man on a jury who's sot agin hangin' when that's all yer want ter git done, can yer? So we was a-tryin' of him fair, with ole man Strong for foreman 'cause he knowed all the forms, as he was out to the hangin' of Howard an' that thief over to Jacksonville an' mos' on 'em. He was pertikler to do it all straight 'cordin' to law, an' we was gittin' 'long slick, when Mis' Weston come an' bust it all up. She said she lent him the hoss, an' it war hern."

The narrator stopped to observe the effect of this announcement. He felt repaid.

"I don't believe it," sobbed Uncle David.

"I hearn her say it," said the man. His complete enjoyment of the effect was marred by the tears of that poor old man.

"We had to let him off, o' course, for the stealin', an' we couldn't hang him for the shootin' o' Jake Mills, 'cause some o' the boys said they'd never hang on nigger evidence, an' we hadn't none other. Anyhow, that nigger he drowned hisself in lies right away, an' we didn't lay much on what he done tole us, you bet. But we was powerful sorry a'terwards when we seen what we'd done. She's gone off with him plumb."

"No, no, not that," said Uncle David, "tain't so, you didn't un'erstan'."

"We axed her war she a-gwine with him, an' she said, 'yes,' I hearn her say so."

"She was on'y goin' home," said Uncle David tremulously.

"She had not come home half an hour ago," observed Madame.

"They rode 'long to the South Fork, an' that don't lie on her road home from Union Mills, do it? I stayed behin' at the Store, the boys was talkin' if they hadn't bes' go right a'ter him an' shoot him anyhow, but we 'lowed he'd ha' showed fight then, an' maybe she'd ha' been killed in the shootin'. Yer can't never say who'll be hit when everybody's firin' like blazes. I didn't quit the Mills for a spell, an' mos' the boys was 'ready gone home, an' they allowed I oughter tell yer we done our best for yer."

They thanked him, and he went his way.

"Somebody has got to tell Brother Ezra, he will be coming home to-night," said the blacksmith, wiping his sleeve across his forehead. "Poor Ezra! What a home-coming!"

Brother Green remained silent for a long time, then he spoke again in a soft low voice, almost as if he was communing with himself.

"When I laid my young wife in her grave with her babe on her breast, fifteen years ago last Midsummer, I thought I had known the greatest sorrow possible to the human heart. But my loss was not so great as Brother Ezra's, his cup is filled to the brim, and oh, how bitter! How great a power of suffering lies in the human heart!"

"It is through suffering that the heart is purified," said Madame to him in reply.

"Aye, so they say: but some sorts of sorrow may very well embitter. People talk of the purifying by sorrow. It seems to me that happiness can purify too. We are all sure to get our share of the sorrow in this world, it is the happiness that so seldom comes to a man. Brother Ezra was happy, is happy, poor man, since he does not yet know of the wreck of his home. It was a delight to see him so happy. And she, poor young thing, my heart aches for her! She was in my forge the other day, said she was lonesome and came to talk. Poor child! We are all to blame. Why did we leave her alone? Why didn't I think of going to see her, instead of merely remembering how bright she was in the forge. We should have looked after her. Madame, why didn't you do so? You are the chief." Brother Green's voice had a stern ring in it, that immensely surprised Madame in her self-contained calm.

"I!" she exclaimed hastily. "I had absolutely no control over her, and no influence. She was one of the most determined young women I ever knew, and the least liable to yield to the judgment of others."

"No, I don't think that was her character," said Brother Green.

"You are taken by the pretty face, like Brother Ezra, and are utterly ignorant of the mind within. Men are always like that in regard to a pretty woman," said Madame scornfully.

"Beauty is a great power, no doubt," admitted Brother Green, "but people may err just as widely by judging everything from the prejudiced point of view as by yielding too far to favourable impressions."

"Brother Green," said Uncle David earnestly, "I'm right glad you're like me, you won't believe nothin' 'gainst little Ollie, will you, no more than I will?"

"I will hope for the best and that there may be some reasonable explanation of her disappearance," said Brother Green, looking compassionately at the piteous old face that scanned his so eagerly for some scrap of comfort.

"I don't see what explanation there can be but the one we have already received," said Madame icily.

"Who will break this sorrowful news to Ezra?" asked Brother Green. "Will you do it, Uncle David? You would do it tenderly, as you have faith in her still."

"No, no, I couldn't bear to see the look o' death in his eyes, an' it 'ud come no matter how I told it, when I came to sayin' little Ollie was gone an' we didn't know where."

"I think perhaps I had best take this painful duty upon myself," suggested Madame.

"Well, after all, maybe you are the best person. But remember to deal tenderly with him in his sorrow. You will know what to say to instil some hope into his heart," said Brother Green sadly.

"An' don't you tell him she's gone off with that man Cotterell, for she hain't done no such thing," said Uncle David anxiously. "You jes' say we don't know why she went away, an' kinder hint as you're expectin' she'll be home to-morrow or nex' day. Do you understand?"

Madame told no one what she would say to Ezra, and made no promises as to how she would say it.

## CHAPTER XX.

#### MADAME'S SYMPATHY.

When Madame saw the white covers of the returning waggons creeping across the prairie she set out to meet Ezra in order to deliver her message to him. Her manner was as quiet and collected as ever, her white smooth brow was perfectly unruffled, and her blue eyes were as gentle in expression as her friends had ever known them to be. Was her heart in reality as calm as her outward appearance would have led the casual observer to conclude? No one ever knew what was passing in Madame's mind. Still she must have known that she was about to stab to the heart a man upon whose friendship she had seemed to set great value. Having reached the slope over Weddell's Gully, whence she could see that blackened field where she had saved Ezra on the night of the fire, she sat down and waited until his waggon came up.

"Ah, Madame!" said he cheerily, as he pulled up. "How glad I am to get home again! It has seemed such a long four days to me."

"And to us also," answered Madame.

"All well, I hope," said Ezra reaching down his hand in order to help her up to the seat beside himself.

"We have had misfortunes at Perfection City. The brown mare has been stolen."

"What! Queen Katharine gone, and our most valuable animal too! That is indeed a loss!"

"Just wait a few minutes," said she, putting her hand on his to stop him from giving the signal to the horses to start on again. "I have some things to talk about, Ezra. Do you remember that night, not long ago in reality, though it seems an age, when I found you lying here on the edge of the fire?"

"Is it likely I could ever forget that or who it was came to my rescue?" said Ezra warmly.

"I was thinking as you drove up that perhaps it would have been a kinder act to have left you to die in your unconsciousness."

"What's the matter?" said Ezra, greatly startled by her words.

"I have bad news," said Madame.

"Is it Olive?" asked Ezra, hoarsely.

"Yes, it is Olive."

"Is she ill?"

"Worse than that."

"My God, is my wife dead?" cried Ezra in a stifled whisper.

"Worse than that."

"There can't be worse," said Ezra,

"Yes, there can. She has left you and gone off with Cotterell."

Ezra threw up his arms and fell backwards. Madame thought for a moment or two that he was dying, for an awful blue-purple look passed over his face as if his heart had stopped beating. He recovered himself and sat up, turned ghastly white, and moved his lips. He was trying to speak, but no sound came. At length he gasped,

"Olive, Olive, where is she?"

"We don't know. Cotterell took the brown mare, the men turned out and caught him. Olive disappeared, no one knew where, night before last, taking our last horse. There was a sort of lynch-law trial at Union Mills, she appeared in the middle of the proceedings and said she gave him the horse, and then they went off together and have not since been heard of."

"Olive, Olive, Olive!" Ezra kept moaning as Madame drove him back to his deserted home. He seemed dazed and stupefied.

Surely terrible news was never more crudely broken to a sufferer than was his bereavement to Ezra Weston, and by that tender and sympathetic friend, Madame Morozoff-Smith. Had Uncle David or Brother Green heard her, they would have been shocked beyond measure at having entrusted the painful embassy to such hands. Not one word of hope or comfort or of doubt even, nothing but the bald hideous story in its worst complexion thrown at him.

Olive was gone from him—gone with Cotterell! Yet after having thus dealt him a death-blow, Madame seemed full of pity and little acts of personal attention. She helped him out of the waggon, brought him into the house, took his hands and washed them, cooled his forehead with a wet towel, offered him food, and in short treated him much as if he had been a suffering child whom she was tending. At last he seemed to recover himself somewhat as she was passing her soft hand across his brow.

"You are very good to me," he said brokenly, "and if I seem to accept your kindness unheedingly, forgive me. I am not myself to-night. I don't know what I am doing. Oh, it can't be!" he suddenly burst out. "She is not gone. I shall see her again. She will come back. How do you know she has gone with him? I don't believe it."

"Poor Ezra, love dies hard, I know. Some of the men asked if she was going with him, and she answered distinctly, 'Yes.' Then they were sorry, they said, they had not hung him before she came up with them."

"No, I won't believe it. Something has happened to her. Why should she go off with him?" said Ezra distractedly.

"Did you not know that he was repeatedly here to see her, whenever you were out of the way?" said

Madame, who did not think she was exaggerating in any way.

"She told me all that," answered Ezra nervously, "but she was only amused by his talk."

"No, your love is blind. Dear Ezra, I wish I could soften the blow. There is no doubt about it. I saw them once together at the spring, he kissed her at parting. It was a man and the woman he loved. I cannot be mistaken. Remember he was very handsome and winning in his manners, and she was young and pretty."

"Ah, my sweet little Ollie! My little rose-bud," cried Ezra, starting to his feet. "I'll go to her, she shall not wander away out of my reach without one effort to save her from herself. She was only a child. Why didn't you look after her?" he asked, suddenly facing Madame with an angry glance.

"Did you give her into my charge either by word or hint?" returned she, somewhat taken aback.

"It was not your fault. Forgive me. I am too distracted to know what I say. I remember she refused to go to you. She said she would rather stay at home. I tried to urge her, but she would not consent to it," said Ezra in a low voice.

"Ah," remarked Madame, "very possibly she expected him to come to her during your absence."

"No, no, you shall not say that!" said Ezra in agony. "I cannot bear it. She had no such thought. She was as innocent as the flowers, as she looked at me with her sweet eyes. She had no such thought, I know."

"It is ever thus," said Madame, coming closer to him and speaking with an unwonted tremor in her voice. "Love seems always at cross purposes. You give all your love to Olive, who gives all hers to Cotterell. Another gives all her love to you. We are equally unhappy."

Ezra gazed at her in silent amazement as if he were doubting that he had understood her.

"Yes," she went on more calmly in her deep sweet voice. "I am more in need of pity than you. Your love has left you, and you grieve, but men will give you sympathy. When I lost my love I had to smile and pretend delight. I had to look on his joy and hers. You are not called upon to congratulate Cotterell on his happiness."

"Great God, is that you, Madame? Or is it that I am going mad, and is this some mocking fiend?" gasped Ezra, starting up.

"Not a mocking fiend, Ezra, but I myself who for once in this world am enjoying the rare privilege of telling the truth. Ezra Weston, you are not the most unhappy person in Perfection City. I have long enjoyed that melancholy pre-eminence. Now in a common misfortune let us comfort one another."

Ezra sat down again and dropped his head in his hands. Occasionally he looked at her as she moved about the room putting everything in order. It almost seemed as if he was trying to understand who she was and that he could hardly do so, his mind was in such a turmoil of grief and misery. She laid out two more candles beside those already alight in the candle-sticks.

"You will sit up all night," she said at last. "These candles will last half the time, then light the other two. It is hard sitting in the dark alone with one's breaking thoughts. Light the candles and keep them burning. That is what I did on the night you left to go to Smyrna to be married, and on the night when you brought her home here to Perfection City."

She closed the door and left him alone with those two thoughts. Was it her marvellous reading of the human heart which prompted this extraordinary woman to declare her love to Ezra in those bold uncompromising words on this night of all others in his life? She knew that he would sit there in his deserted home, brooding over his lost wife, she knew also that every now and then the scorching recollection of what she had said would break in upon the brooding thoughts and scatter them. This then was the means, the almost unheard-of means, she had taken in order to soften the blow that had fallen upon him. He would not be able to think of himself as the most unhappy individual in Perfection City, because she had claimed that distinction in words which he never could forget. It was just as she had foreseen. It repeatedly happened during the course of that long and dreadful night that Ezra forgot why he was sitting alone in the kitchen, so lost was he in amazement at the recollection of the words which Madame had spoken. As the hours wore on it seemed to him that they became more and more impossible, until he began to think of them as the work of a brain unhinged by sorrow. Was it all a hideous dream, and would he awake by and bye? The first pair of candles burned out, and he lighted the second pair, recalling as he did so what she had said she did when he brought Olive home. Ah, Olive, Olive! His heart kept calling out in its misery.

He went into their little private room off the kitchen, in a sort of infatuation to see if she might be there. No. All was silent, still, deserted. He examined the tiny room minutely, saw the half-withered flowers on the table, took them up, and would have kissed them in his misery, only his eye lighted on a strange object he had never seen before. It was a man's heavy seal-ring. He picked it up and examined it by the light of the candle: a plain gold ring set with a well-cut onyx intaglio of a griffin's head. As he turned it about the light showed something engraved in the inside of the ring. He held the candle nearer and read "J. G. C."

He dropped the ring as if it had been an adder, and fled out of the room. As if pursued by furies, he rushed from the house and wandered about out of doors. Diana, who since Olive's departure had been in a most miserable frame of mind, followed him about dejectedly, with her tail between her legs. Ezra, turning, saw the dog and for one moment felt a savage desire to kill it, for Olive had loved the dog and Olive had broken his heart. This phase passed, and in a passion of grief and despair he stooped and kissed the animal, for Olive had often patted Diana's head, and fondled her long ears. The dog whined in sympathy and turned suggestively back to the house. Ezra followed mechanically. He would not go into the room where that ring lay, but remained in the kitchen. Exhausted nature could stand no more, and towards morning he fell into a troubled sleep, with his head resting upon his arms crossed on the table. Then in his dreams Olive came back to him in that vivid yet unsatisfying way in which our dearest do sometimes return to us, seemingly but to mock our grief. Olive was there, standing before him, but she looked at him not with her eyes, but with Madame's. There was something terrible in seeing her own expression gone and in its place the look of another, and yet it was Olive, and she called on him to follow her. He hurried after her with the lead-clogged feet that always walk in dreams, and strained to reach her. When he did so, he found Madame. Olive and Madame flitted before his fevered fancy, always shifting and changing one into another, until he panted with the horror of it.

He awoke with a start as the door opened. His

half-aroused eyes saw a vaguely defined figure in the door-way, blocking out the light of the morning.

"Olive," he said, putting out his hand blindly.

"I have come to cook your breakfast," said Madame's soft smooth voice.

"Don't. I can't eat it," said Ezra, falling back into despair.

"Life must go on, even when all joy is banished from it," she said. "We have each one of us to learn that lesson, friend Ezra."

She began deftly enough to light the fire and make the necessary preparations for breakfast. Madame knew how to do the ordinary house-work that falls to woman's lot, only she did not choose to do it in her own home. Therefore she employed Lucinda for this purpose, until other and stronger motives arose which prompted her to undertake the work herself. The habit of every-day life is strong, and when Ezra saw Madame getting breakfast ready, as a matter of course he arose and got himself ready, by changing his clothes and generally performing the necessary preliminaries to the morning meal. He was less wild and hollow-eyed after this ceremony, but the extraordinary drawn and aged look on his face seemed only the more marked.

Madame cooked an omelette with scraps of savoury dried beef in it, and after the first mouthful Ezra was obliged to admit that he relished the food. He could not go on living on his grief, as Madame said.

She sat with him and took her breakfast also. Napoleon Pompey, who would have been in the way, was relegated to the society of his mother, who divided her emotions between maternal anger at boyish shortcomings and maternal love for the short-comer, both of which were expressed with the exalted vehemence customary to the negro nature.

"I shall come each day and cook your food for you. I have often longed to be able to do something for you, Ezra. Do not forbid my coming. I have had so little joy in my life," said Madame, with a strange humility of manner totally at variance with her usual character, which was almost domineering, one might say. Ezra looked at her in a troubled sort of way. It soothed him to have her there, and he was glad that somebody, that anybody, could take an interest in him. Still there came across his mind flashes of doubt as to what this interest meant. He could not forget those words that Madame had used on the evening before. No man who had ever heard such words from a woman's lips, if ever man did hear them under similar circumstances, would ever again be able to drive them from his memory, but in his bruised and suffering state Ezra was content to drift on and let things rest. So Madame came daily to his house and cooked his food and saw that he ate something at each meal.

Uncle David and the brethren came to see him, but that gave him no comfort. He shrank from their sympathy, expressed with kindness, but each word was like a drop of molten lead upon a raw wound. Willette was perhaps the only one who gave him real consolation in this awful time.

"I say," remarked the child, in a clear voice and without a trace of embarrassment, "Sister Ollie's gone an' lost herself down there in the bush, I reckon. She was 'bout the greenest hand at keepin' to the Pole Star ever I see. You could throw her out o' her direction quicker nor nothin'. I guess she headed plumb for the Missouri border when she come 'long with Cotterell to show him out o' Union Mills. Guess she'll ride 'bout down to Saint Jo 'fore she knows she's headin' wrong. I wouldn't 'spect her back 'fore a fortnight." Willette laughed pleasantly, and poor Ezra derived some comfort from the preposterous convictions of the child and her unshakable belief in Olive.

He went to Union Mills to make some inquiries about his lost wife, and met there the same story that Madame had already told, but the story was so brutally hurled at him he could not bear it, and came home bruised and stricken, his heart bleeding tears of agony. Instinctively he went to Madame for comfort.

"Ezra, perhaps this terrible trial was needed to purify us all, to make us all more perfect communists. I can discern a valuable lesson that may be of profit to the brethren. I begin to think that after all marriage is selfish: perfect love alone is unselfish. You would not have kept Olive beside you by force, if her heart had gone from you, would you?"

"I thought our marriage was for life."

"Yes, but she made a mistake as to her feelings; she found she loved someone else better. It was wise of her, after all, to break the bond. It would only have galled you both."

"I should have been content if she had only let me love her," said Ezra.

"Ah yes, I know that feeling but too well," said Madame, bringing his mind with a shock to the thought that she never long allowed to sleep.

"It is a terrible world," said Ezra beginning to realize what a spell she was weaving around him.

"It rests with ourselves to make it easier in the only way," replied Madame.

Uncle David took up a firm position of his own and refused to listen to anybody or anything.

"I hain't a-goin' to b'lieve nothin' 'gin little Ollie," he announced. "I don't care 'bout proofs an' things. Land! If I b'lieved in proofs there hain't no sort o' foolishness I shouldn't be up to. I b'lieve in pussons."

That was his position, and he stuck to it with unswerving fidelity. He was happy in his blind faith, and no one tried to shake it. The old man then began a strange sort of hunt after Olive. He would sit all day long at the forge, where, of course, strangers were most likely to pass, and to each he would put questions about the "little gal" he was so pathetically seeking. He spoke little, he who used to be so chatty, but sat hour after hour in silent patient expectation of the return of his loved one. The brethren began to think he must be losing his wits from sorrow, poor old man!

# CHAPTER XXI.

### THE MESSAGE.

A LONG weary fortnight had passed since the day when Ezra came home to find his wife gone. Life went on at Perfection City much the same as before, although to him it seemed as if the Universe was out of gear. He took no part or interest in the daily affairs of the Community, never coming to the Assembly or consulting with the brethren upon any matters. He withdrew himself from the companionship of his fellows, and only that Madame continued to come to his house every day in order to cook his dinner and sit with him while he ate it, he would have been absolutely alone. Ezra acquiesced in her devotion, and dared not ask himself how the debt was to be repaid that she was piling up against him. The Pioneers, who during the past fortnight had revelled in a perfect carnival of gossip, felt themselves at liberty to express an opinion upon this new development of the drama that was being acted in their midst. Sister Carpenter said to Sister Winkle that she thought there ought to be a period of mourning allowed, however brief, between first and second marriage, and that Brother Ezra hadn't ought to go a-courting so soon. She did not know that it was Madame who did the courting in that strange, forward, imperial way that we must suppose the Empress Katharine affected. Uncle David, whom love for Olive had rendered extremely keen-sighted as to what was going on, evinced very great displeasure. Madame had no right to try and make Ezra's home happy, and he told her so in language of unmistakable import. She was angry to a degree that terrified him, and he shrank back alarmed beyond measure at the wrath which he had provoked.

"Yes, I know, you want Ezra's life to be wrecked by that vain, selfish little hussy who never cared for him, and who went off with the first gallant that beckoned to her. Ezra's life shall not be wrecked, mine shall be expended in drawing it into a haven of rest. Olive is not worthy of tying the latchet of his shoe. I hope she will be cast off by her lover, and left to sink amid the mud and mire of such as she. I hate her!"

Uncle David was frightened and crept away to Brother Green, where he sat hour after hour mournfully watching the fire. It was on one of these days when he was in the forge that a young negro on a raw-boned Indian pony rode up to Madame, who was on the point of starting for her daily expedition to Ezra's, and inquired "whar ole man Weston lived," as he had a message for him. Instead of answering directly, Madame endeavoured to find out what the boy wanted of Ezra. The little darkie thereupon produced a scrap of crumpled paper from the recesses of his ragged shirt and informed Madame he wanted to give him " dat ar'." Madame took the paper, opened it, and gave a gasp. Then in a moment she recovered herself with an effort, and assured the negro it was all right, and that she would see to it. She made most particular inquiries as to where he lived, and then sent him off, happy with a piece of corn-bread and a dollar for himself.

Having thus got rid of the negro lad, Madame proceeded on her way to Ezra's house in order to perform her daily task there. She seemed strangely excited, and her blue eyes glittered like sapphires. Her whole bearing was that of a person labouring under intense excitement, all traces of which she was endeavouring to conceal. Her very voice had a new ring in it as she talked with Ezra, and her breath came quick and fast. Had his senses been less dulled by suffering, he could not have failed to notice the change in her, notwithstanding her efforts at concealment. He was sitting, looking with unseeing eyes across the vacant cornfield, when suddenly she spoke.

" Ezra, let us go away from this place. Let us leave all the recollections of Perfection City behind us, and begin life afresh."

He turned his eyes upon her with a slow questioning look, showing how far away had been his thoughts at the moment.

"How can we leave this place? There is too much money and too much labour sunk in it for us all to leave and go to some other spot."

"Not all, dear friend, only you and I," said Madame, in her caressing voice.

Ezra started. "That is even more impossible," he said, in great agitation.

"Why impossible? I have money. It will more than suffice for all our needs, nay, it will give us all the luxuries we can sigh for."

"It is not that, but you forget——"

"No, Ezra, I don't forget, but I want you to forget. I want you to draw a wet sponge over the recollection of the past and begin anew. It is not too late."

"You don't know what you are saying, Madame. You cannot mean it."

"I do mean it, and I know what it means. You have no tie——"

Ezra shivered.

"Neither have I. We are both free to make our lives what we list."

"You mistake, we are both tied by all our past lives, and with bonds that may not be lightly broken. We are tied by our own feelings as well as by the good opinion of the world at large."

Madame snapped her fingers with scorn.

"That for the world at large and its opinions.

Do you remember what I told you about my father and my birth? Thank God, I have no name to lose."

"I cannot do less than tell you the truth," said Ezra in great distress. "Wherever I went my heart would remain here, where I have known true happiness, and it will always be looking for my lost one to come back to me."

"She won't come back till Cotterell is tired of her," said Madame brutally. "Will you be grateful for his cast-off mistress?"

"Stop," said Ezra, putting his hand quickly before her lips, "you must not speak so of her to me."

"Fool that I am!" muttered Madame under her breath. She turned from him with a gesture of anger.

"Oh, forgive me," exclaimed Ezra, seeing and feeling what the expression meant. "Never was man so miserable, never was one so unhappily placed. I owe you more than words can say, I owe you my best thoughts, I owe you my very life itself. I would willingly give you my life——"

"Then why not give it and come with me?" burst out Madame. "Leave all this misery behind you, I will make your path as smooth as heart could wish. Come."

"My heart can never follow any other path, it will dwell amid the ruins of its former happiness. Do not speak again of this. Let us remain friends as before."

"It can never be again as it was before," said Madame with heaving bosom.

"Why not?" asked Ezra. "I have not much else left in life."

"Why not," repeated Madame in scorn. "You ask me why not! Would you care for Olive's friendship when all her love was given to Cotterell?"

"Stop," cried Ezra, and this time there was a ring of anger in his voice. "Even you may presume too far. Do not again speak that name to me."

There is something untamed and untameable in the Russian nature which now and then comes to the surface and drives an excited Muscovite into acts seemingly at variance with the highly cultivated standard to which he aspires. The phenomenon may by the learned be attributed to a sudden reversion to the ancestral Asiatic savage. Madame was at this moment rapidly going back to the state of furious anger, when all sense of dignity would be lost. She was reverting to the Asiatic. And under the influence of her passion her physical appearance changed, her eyes became narrow slanting openings emitting sparks of steel-blue flame, her full red lips were drawn tightly over her teeth. She hissed out her words.

"Does her image still come between us?"

"It does come between us," said Ezra looking almost as white as she did. "Her image will always come between me and every other woman on the whole earth, blotting out every other image and making me only hers. Oh, Olive! Oh, my wife!"

He gave a great sob of agony.

"Besotted fool!" burst from Madame's colourless lips, "do you hold this language to me? You scorn me and my love! Then on your own head be the consequences. Ah, now nothing shall stop me. An angel from heaven, no, nor God Himself shall stand between me and my revenge. Ezra Weston, farewell!"

She left the room, shutting the door upon him and his misery. Unhappy man! His world seemed crumbling beneath his feet. He had lost his wife, and now his friend, the one whom he most revered, had cast him out from her regard. What could he do? His heart answered, nothing but dumbly suffer in the deserted home where he was left alone. What a black and barren waste was his life! And how fair and smiling it had looked a few short weeks ago! It was as if a devastating fire had passed over him leaving his heart like the desolated prairie, black and hopeless.

Madame went away alone for one day, no one knew whither, and came back with a look on her face that struck terror into all who saw her. Her smooth white face looked cruel and pitiless, and the gleam from her eyes reminded one of cold steel. Her soft hands sometimes closed on their own pink palms with a spasmodic clutch, as if she had the throat of an enemy between their cruel grasp and was crushing the life out of him. A cold dreadful face, a cruel sickening look that made Napoleon Pompey and Uncle David shiver within their souls, and caused the brethren to draw away affrighted from their once beloved leader. Perfection City was the abode of wretchedness. The Academy never opened its doors to the assembled Pioneers, who were afraid to come near Madame's house. Each lived by himself, looking askance at his neighbour, for over all had fallen a spirit of suspicion. Only Brother Huntley, the deaf brother, and his mute wife were happy, working on contentedly, shielded by their misfortune from the full knowledge of the disasters that had come upon the Community.

The days dragged miserably by, seemingly endowed with a miraculous length of hours, for the sufferings of a life-time were compressed into that hideous fortnight. The glaring sun blazing down upon the blackened prairie seemed to Ezra to have become no unfitting symbol of hell. The light was hateful, darkness, eternal darkness would have been a relief to his brain. Could it be possible that he was going to live his life out in a realized purgatory? He was young, only twenty-five, and if his life was to stretch even to the average span of human existence, what an eternity of suffering lay before him! A broken-hearted man amid the ruins of his broken life.

It was on one of these days of utter black despair, like the days that had gone before and the days that were still to come, that the same ragged negro boy on the straggly Indian pony, who once before had made his appearance at Perfection City, was seen skulking around the old land near Weddell's Gully. He seemed to want to see without being seen. By and bye Napoleon Pompey chanced that way and of course pounced upon him with the universal query of " whar he gwine?" The boy after some hesitation made it clear that he had come on a secret mission. He wanted to find Uncle David without being seen by anyone else, especially not by the white-faced lady, Madame, of whom he stood in shivering dread. Napoleon Pompey, sympathising with the dread, volunteered to take a letter to Uncle David without fear of detection. Thereupon the darkie delivered over to him a scrap of newspaper upon which was written a scrawl with the burnt end of a stick, and having done so galloped off on his straggly pony with a whoop of delight, as one who had escaped dreadful peril. Napoleon Pompey, finding it difficult to deliver his embassy to Uncle David undetected, gave the curious missive to Ezra with intimations that it was to be put into Uncle David's hands right away.

Ezra took the scrap of paper, saying there must be some letter inside, and mechanically unfolded it, when the hoarse scream that he uttered almost made Napoleon Pompey jump through the window.

" Where did you get this?" he panted.

" Darkie gin it ter me jes' while back."

"Who gave it? What was his name? Where did he live? Who sent him here?" asked Ezra in a breath.

"Darkie he didn't go for to say nuffin, on'y jes' gin dat ar, an' tole me ter pike to ole Uncle David wid it."

Ezra darted out of the house and ran like a madman to Madame's and burst into the room where she and Uncle David were just sitting down to supper. He held out the scrap of paper to the old man and gasped:

"Olive is somewhere!"

"I presume that was already known, and that it can hardly be considered news," said Madame's cool cutting voice, which brought Ezra somewhat to his senses.

"She is somewhere near. She sent a negro boy with this. Read it." He shoved it under Uncle David's nose.

"I can't see to read it, read it aloud, let me hear all she says in her letter," said the old man with trembling eagerness.

"It isn't a letter. It says, 'Uncle come to Olive,' only those four words, nothing else, and just look, scratched with a bit of burnt stick on a piece of newspaper! Oh, think of it! Where can she be? Why didn't she write before if she was in trouble? What has happened?"

"Perhaps it is a hoax," said Madame between her drawn white lips.

"There hain't in this world a bein' so lost to all feelin' as would make a joke o' our sorrow," said Uncle David. "No, Ezra, that's writ by our little gal. We must go to her. Come 'long, brother." He put on his hat and started cheerfully for the door.

"Where are you going?" asked Madame, in a muffled voice.

"I'm a-goin' to little Ollie."

"Where is she, do you know?"

"Ezry, don't you know where we've got to go to?"

"I know nothing, except that this scrap of paper has been brought by a negro boy."

Ezra kissed the paper, and Madame's lips curled in contempt.

"Is it not rather a wild-goose chase to start you know not whither, and at this time of the evening too?"

"We can't wait here after little Ollie's told us to come," said Uncle David simply.

"Cannot you suggest some plan?" asked Ezra, turning to Madame by force of habit.

"Not I," she replied contemptuously. "Shall you go east, west, north, or south? The world lies all before you."

"Ain't you glad little Ollie's found?" asked Uncle David, looking wistfully at her.

Madame laughed harshly. They went out of the room together feeling her presence insupportable.

Just round the corner they came upon Napoleon Pompey who was peeping around to see if he could pick up any scraps of news. He had divined there was news from Olive, and with the inquisitiveness of his race had followed Ezra when he had rushed so wildly out of the house.

"D'yer know whar ter go?" he inquired.

"No," said Ezra. "Can you tell us anything of that negro boy? Do you know where he lives?"

"Ask her," said Napoleon Pompey, jerking his thumb over his shoulder in the direction of the door from which they had just emerged.

"Ask who?"

"Madame," said Napoleon Pompey.

"Does she know?" asked Ezra, amazed.

"I seed dat ar pony hyar afore," replied Napoleon Pompey.

"Great Heavens!" said Ezra as drops of sweat burst out on his forehead. He hurried back to the house with Uncle David. Neither of them spoke a word.

"Madame," said Ezra, as they once more stood in the room, "I have come to ask you a question. Do you know where my wife is?"

She looked him unflinchingly in the face and answered:

"Yes."

"May the Lord forgive you!" said Uncle David, in a voice hardly above a whisper, and for some seconds there was a complete silence in the room, broken only by the sound of Ezra's heavy breathing.

"Where is she?" he demanded sternly.

"Go and find her," was the mocking answer.

Ezra sprang furiously forward, and almost yelled out,

"Tell me at once or——"

"Ay yes," she said with a steady look, "you will drag the secret out, will you?"

She tore open her dress and exposed her snow-white throat.

"See, there it is handy. Take a knife and cut my throat. See if I shall flinch. The last gurgle of my blood bubbling up through the wound, shall bear a sound of mocking laughter. Strike!"

Ezra turned from her in horror. "She must be mad," he said to Uncle David.

"Not mad now, I have been mad all these months, all these years. Mad to love you, mad in loving such a one as you. Now I am sane. Ah, how I hate you!"

"This is horrible," said Ezra, putting his hand before his eyes.

"Horrible, is it? It is the waking from love's young dream. Ha, ha!"

"Madame, dear child, think of all you have been to us," said Uncle David, reaching his hands out to her imploringly. "You have led us, think of all that."

"I do think of all that. I think of how I found this boy," she said, pointing in scorn to Ezra, "ignorant, unformed, with wild crude longings. I think of how I infused light and life into the darkness of his mind. How I rose, aye, above myself, in order to lead him up and on. I think of all his half-formed longings put into working form and endowed with vital power that he might see his thoughts taking shape. I made him. He was mine. Then he left me for a few brief weeks. He saw a pretty doll's face with an empty head, and straightway he loves with never a thought of me. You ask me to think. I do think of how even this I bore, and so great was my love that for his sake I welcomed the doll that had stolen my place, and smiled on her. Even this I did and remained his friend. She, the doll, attracted by a handsome face, her love aroused by the stolen kisses of a yellow moustache, left him. Then I was free to love him once more. I laid my heart at his feet. He spurned me. All my love was as nothing against the memory of the doll who had deserted him. She may die and rot before word of mine shall restore her to him."

Neither Ezra nor Uncle David had attempted to speak while Madame was pouring forth the torrent of her bitter words. Ezra felt too overwhelmed to say anything, for a moment, in the downfall of so many illusions and high hopes, he forgot even Olive. Uncle David was the first to recover himself.

"Dear child," he said, for the first time in his life addressing her as one beneath him. "These are wild words you've been sayin'. I can't find it in my heart to believe they're true. You are disappointed, an' you think wrong can be made right by turnin' things upside down. Tain't so. You'll have to learn that right an' wrong can't change places, nohow you fix it. You have still your duty here in the City you've founded an' the principles you've set up."

Madame looked at him with glittering eyes.

"Will you hear the truth about Perfection City too? Then listen. It is not an experiment in new principles, it is an example of the oldest the world has seen—of the folly of a fond woman. I founded Perfection City so that he might love the founder. I staked my all on a throw of love's dice, and lost. Women have done it before and will do it again. Some fools degrade their body to win a man, I degraded my mind. The foundation-stone of Perfection City was my heart, see what will happen when it is crushed! Ah, why can we not profit by the experience of our elders! My mother warned me, having tried it, never to stake my happiness on the love of man. I followed her advice for five-and-thirty happy years. Then I saw *him*, and the curse fell."

She threw up her arms over her head and backed towards the door of her own apartment.

"The curse, the curse!" she exclaimed, as she passed through out of their sight.

Ezra had a confused feeling that he had just seen someone drowning who had reached appealing hands towards heaven as she went under.

## CHAPTER XXII.

#### OLIVE'S SECOND HOME-COMING.

AND where was Olive all this time? She and Cotterell rode out of Union Mills together, as we have seen, and as was seen by nearly all the men who had assembled there that morning in the expectation of seeing him hanged. They rode silently among "the boys" getting their horses ready, they silently passed among the trees to the south and crossed the ford of the Creek. Then Cotterell spoke, pouring forth his words of thanks and gratitude to her. He was not ashamed to show that he was deeply moved, now that none but Olive could see his emotion. She, on the other hand, seemed almost in an unconscious state so little heed did she give to his eager words.

"Speak to me, tell me what you wish," he pleaded very gently, noticing her abstraction.

"I want you to go away," she said slowly. "You are safe from their anger for this time, but do not stay here and court danger. This is no place for a man like you to live. Go while there is yet time. There is now a blood-feud between you and the Mills.

They will mark you for vengeance, and they are wild bad men."

"And you?" said Cotterell, looking anxiously at her. "I want to see you safely at home. You are ill, I fear."

"I am all right," answered Olive wearily. "You must go to the South Fork at once. Take the Kansas City stage this very night and go. There is no time to be lost."

"I cannot, and will not," answered Cotterell. "I must take you home first. You look frightfully tired and ill."

"No, it would be the cruelest thing you could do to bring me home. I want to go back to Ezra, I am so tired," said Olive plaintively.

"Must I let you go all by yourself over this lonely prairie? I cannot bear the thought of it."

"I have been two days and one night all by myself out on this lonely prairie in order to save you. Please do what I ask. Tie Queen Katharine's rein to Rebel's bit, they will then go quietly together."

"Tell me," said Cotterell breathlessly, "why have you been out all this time on the prairie alone?"

"I was following the men who had captured you in order to save you if I could."

"Great Heavens!" he burst out, with his blue eyes aflame. "And you did this heroic act because you——"

"I did it because you are an innocent man, and

I wanted you to go back to your country to live a better life and be a better man than you ever had been before."

The light died out of his eyes. He looked down, his hands trembled as they had never trembled when on his trial.

"Your sacrifice shall not have been in vain," he said in a low voice.

"Then good-bye, and all good blessings attend you."

She shook hands with him and left him standing at the parting of the ways. When she was quite out of sight over the ridge on her way towards Cotton Wood Creek, he, with blinding tears streaming down his sun-burnt face, turned and walked to the South Fork, caught the Kansas City stage-coach and departed out of Olive's life.

She hardly knew what she was doing she felt so ill. It seemed a relief not to have to talk any more, for she found it difficult to keep hold of her thoughts, they seemed constantly to be slipping away from her. The sun was burning hot, and she had a long way to go, for she had come out of Union Mills by the south side instead of the north. Therefore she must make a great sweep round to the right in order to reach her home, and she must remember that the Creek was only to be safely forded at certain places. She rode on and on, feeling the sun hotter and hotter and her head heavier and heavier. At last she was so dizzy she could no longer see where she was going. Whatever happened she must lie down for a few minutes. Somehow she got off her horse and lay down at the side of the track she had been following, but whether in sleep or in unconsciousness she never knew.

By and by she came to herself again. The horses were both gone! She had forgotten to picket them. She did not remember where she was, but mechanically stumbled along the road and at length was overtaken by a negro woman driving an ox-waggon. She begged of the woman to let her get into the waggon and take her home for she felt ill, and the negress, struck with pity, declared she would, " fo' de po' chile was mos' sick to deaf anyhow." Olive got into the waggon and knew no more for hours—or was it days, or was it weeks? Two nights out in the poisonous prairie dew had done their work: she was down with chills and fever, a raving panting lunatic, or else a stupid heavy sleeping log, taking no heed of day or night or the hours as they flew, only craving water to drink, ever more water to drink. By and by she began to have intervals when she knew that she was in a strange place with strange black faces around her. Then at last her senses returned, and she sent an imploring message to Ezra to come to her. In reply had come Madame, stern, fierce-eyed, to see her and crush her with the awful news that Ezra was dead. Olive fell back into unconsciousness under the blow, she did not know for how long. But after weary suffering she awoke again, still in that same strange place, still with those black faces around her, kind and pitying, but faces she did not know.

Trying feebly to gather up again the threads of her life, she wished to send word to the friends at Perfection City that she was still alive. The negroes, who were the only inhabitants of the wretched house where she was, seemed not to heed her wishes. They refused to take any messages, but would not say why. Olive grew stronger, for her young vitality exerted itself. She demanded to know why they would not do as she wished, but they fled from her questions and left her to her suspicions. She tormented them with questions, and at last they said the white-faced lady had forbidden them ever to come near her house again, and they were afraid: she was a very terrible looking lady when she was angry. Then Olive used her powers of persuasion upon the negro lad and eventually got him to take her message in spite of what his mother said. That was the scrap of paper that had come into Ezra's hands.

The Pioneers scattered in systematic search for Olive, spreading out in all directions in a way that could not fail to be speedily successful. Brother Green found her on the second day, while Ezra found the two horses which a thrifty settler had impounded in his own fields and was unobtrusively working until they should be called for by their owner.

Brother Green was overjoyed at finding Olive

and was not so overwhelmed at hearing of her long illness as, under different circumstances, he might have been. In fact he was almost pleased, for that fact, taken together with the negro woman's graphic account of finding her alone and ill on the prairie on the day " o' de hoss-thief tryin'," made it clear to him that she had never been with Cotterell since she was at the abortive trial. She was very weak and languid and took little heed of him or his remarks.

"Ezra will be out of his mind with joy," he said, by way of rousing her to some interest, as he was settling her as comfortably as he could in the ox-waggon, preparatory to setting out on their return.

"Ezra is dead," said Olive wearily.

Brother Green stared hard at her. "What crazy fancy is this? Ezra is alive and riding over towards Jacksonville at this moment hunting for you."

"She told me he was dead," said Olive, beginning to cry from the revulsion of feeling combined with physical suffering.

"How dared the woman tell such a lie!" exclaimed Brother Green angrily, and then after a moment he added more mildly, "Perhaps it was a mere mistake, she seems to have been kind to you, but negroes are not a truth-telling race."

"It was not the negro woman, it was Madame," said Olive in a hushed and awe-struck voice.

"Nonsense, you are raving, Sister Olive," said he sharply.

"She came to me and told me during my illness."

"When?"

"I can't tell. I don't remember when things happened. I was so ill."

"Then depend upon it, you have fancied this. Fever fancies seem very real at times."

He experienced a certain relief in speaking thus confidently on the subject to her.

"The negro woman knows. Ask her who came here and forbade them to bring any more messages from me to Perfection City."

It was singular, considering the way he had spoken, that Brother Green did not take this simple means of assuring himself that Olive's idea was the effect of the disordered workings of a fevered brain. But he said never a word to the negro woman on the subject, but drove slowly and thoughtfully back to Perfection City, with Olive in the ox-waggon, lying on a heap of corn-shucks covered with the ragged patch-quilt the woman had lent her. It was a long and a weary journey thus creeping back home over the blackened prairie. Olive sometimes wondered if she would get there alive, and she moaned in her misery. For the rest, Brother Green spoke but little. Since assuring Olive of the falseness of her idea that Madame had been to see her, he appeared to have lost the cheerfulness he had shown upon finding her. Brother Green was thinking of the future of Perfection City, and it looked black enough to him. It was no secret that Madame had refused to reveal Olive's whereabouts to her husband, and in the light of that circumstance he could foresee nothing but strife, ill-will and enmity in Perfection City. How were Olive and Madame to meet, and above all how were they to live in harmony for the future? These were the thoughts that occupied his mind and kept him silent during that long slow drive.

Olive, too, was trying to look into the future, and she shivered with dread as she did so. Madame's pitiless eyes were before her still, but Ezra would be there, he would shield her and comfort her, and she could rest her head peacefully on his honest breast. Dear Ezra! Why had he not come to her when she had sent for him? She hoped he would be there to greet her and to save her from that terrible woman, whose colourless face in its icy cruelty still haunted her, filling her with a great dread. She need not have been so afraid, for when she reached Perfection City Madame was gone.

The Pioneers had indeed a life of much inward excitement during these days. The return of Olive and the departure of Madame were events almost equally calculated to disturb their equanimity as a Community.

Ezra being still away looking for his wife in the wrong direction, there was no one to receive her when she got home. Therefore Brother Green took her to Sister Mary Winkle's at once on their arrival. Olive was weak, ill, and peevish, she cried with disappointment at not seeing Ezra. Sister Mary Winkle administered a stimulant in the way of advice.

"I wouldn't take on so like a baby, Olive Weston, if I were you. Ezra'll come home probably to-day or to-morrow, and one day more or less ain't much in a life-time."

Olive dried her eyes with energy.

"Everybody said you had gone off with that man Cotterell, and so we all thought too," observed Sister Winkle conversationally.

"How dare you suggest such a thing to me?" exclaimed Olive, with an amount of angry energy surprising in one so weak.

"Well, we had it from the people who saw you go away with him, and who heard you say you were going. I don't see how we could possibly have thought other than we did."

"You must be a wicked woman to think such a thing," said Olive. Her chin began to quiver piteously.

"I am not going to condemn you," replied Sister Winkle, in a philosophic vein. "If you found you preferred him to Ezra I don't think you would have been wrong in showing your preference in an unmistakable manner. Marriage is a partnership which either side should be free to dissolve. Mistakes are sometimes made in it as in other affairs. Our marriage is not a mistake, because Wright and I don't make mistakes, but other people are different, and I don't see why they should be punished for an honest mistake. Marriage should be free. Perfection City was founded on freedom. We thought that you had used your right of choice, and since you liked Cotterell best had gone with him. We thought that Madame would soon marry Ezra, since he was now free, and she had always wanted to."

Olive sprang from her chair and steadied herself with her trembling hands by clutching the back of it.

"Mary Winkle, I hate you," she said, in a voice choking with emotion. "Perfection City is a sinful, wicked place. I wish I had never seen it. If I live, and Ezra loves me, I hope he will take me away so I may never hear its name again."

She stamped bravely out of the house under the influence of her anger, but her strength did not carry her far, and she sank down upon the wood-pile weeping bitterly, unable to walk another step. Sister Mary, somewhat disgusted at the way in which her philosophy had been received, resolved to let her cool off a little before going out to offer Olive an arm to conduct her back into the house. Thus it came about that Olive was still sitting weeping on the wood-pile when Uncle David came hurrying up, having just heard of her arrival, and close behind him came Ezra running like a mad-man. When Olive saw him she started towards her husband with outstretched arms, but her weakness overcame her, and she would have fallen to the ground only that he was just in time to catch her in his arms, where she fell laughing and crying in the most incoherent manner imaginable.

"Oh, Ezra, you didn't believe that wicked story? And you do love me, don't you? And you won't marry her, and you aren't dead, are you? Tell Mary Winkle you hate her too. And why didn't you come to me when I sent for you?"

Ezra could only kiss her, and pet her, and soothe her in every way while Olive kept saying hysterically, "You won't, will you?" and "You will, won't you?" All of which Ezra promised faithfully to perform. She absolutely refused to re-enter Sister Mary Winkle's house, whereupon the latter, somewhat conscience-stricken, offered to send in food for their supper at their own house, provided Olive was not told who had sent it. The secret was kept, and Olive partook heartily of what otherwise would undoubtedly have choked her.

Uncle David hovered over her with anxious love and remorse. "Bless her heart, o' course he didn't b'lieve nothin' 'bout her goin' off. Yer bet he didn't, he knowed it was all right, on'y she was so long a-comin' home he sorter kinder got oneasy, an' that's why they went out to fin' her, an' dear, dear, had she been an' gone an' got that plaguey ague, an' he not there to see a'ter her, an' there wasn't nothin' like Ayre's Ague Cure for that, an' he would go right 'long home this minute an' get her some right away."

Ezra wanted to hear her story, and she told him everything from the beginning to the end. When she came to the end and told him of Madame's visit, he shivered and said it must have been delirium, he bade her think no more of it and never speak of it again. His mind started back from the thoughts such a story raised up before him. He was afraid, and looked away from the abyss, terrified at what lay but half hidden there.

# CHAPTER XXIII.

### CONCLUSION.

MADAME left Perfection City alone and unattended. No one knew that she was going, and no one knew whither she went. Her spirit, however, still hovered over the city of her founding and made itself most potently felt. She sold all her rights in the place, and since these included the land, horses, and implements, as well as most of the houses, the Pioneers awoke in early winter to find themselves homeless and houseless, cast upon the bleak world again. In a tempest of indignation, Sister Mary Winkle and her husband departed out of the place, and after them the Carpenters. The going of the Wrights was highly characteristic. They had managed to save a waggon and a pair of horses out of the general wreck, along with a few of the most primitive household necessaries. These, with his wife and daughter, Brother Wright packed into his waggon and started for Union Mills. At the store there he bought a rifle, a bowie-knife, and a plentiful supply of ammunition. He came out of the store looking like a buccaneer ready equipped for

Central America. Mary Winkle raised her hands in speechless horror.

"I say, pa, be yer goin' to be a jay-hawker?" asked Willette, grinning with delight.

Wright got into the waggon in grim silence.

"What *are* you going to be?" asked Sister Mary recovering her speech at last.

"I'm going to be a man, Mrs. Wright, and not a blamed fool any longer. Guess I'll pre-empt some land near the Cherokee Reservation, and stick to it and get the fruits of my toil, anyhow."

"Your principles——" stammered his wife.

"Damn principles, Mrs. Wright. I've had about enough of them. Common sense is what I want, and so do you. I guess a spell of that will come handy now."

Thus they journeyed out of sight, but a legend came floating back from near the Cherokee lands that at a difficult ford Wright was attacked by a couple of robbers, whereupon he took up that new rifle of his and fired so uncommonly straight that one man fell into the river, and the other ran away.

Brother Green remained at his forge, for blacksmiths were much in request on the prairie, and such a one as he was hard to find. The new owner of Perfection City offered him good inducements to stay, so he stayed. He is still there shoeing horses and mending ploughs. The name has been changed to Mountainburg, in order to emphasise the existence of the rising ground over Weddell's Gully. Brother Green is almost the oldest inhabitant now, and sometimes he thinks of that far-off English village where he was born, and it looks brighter and more beautiful to him as the years roll him away from it. He thinks too of the grass-grown grave in the church-yard where the jackdaws caw overhead, and it seems to him that when his last day's work shall be done he would rest more peacefully beside that mound than in any other spot beneath the broad canopy of heaven.

Brother Dummy decided not to leave when the rest of the Pioneers scattered. He preferred to stay where he was and rent a bit of land from the new owner. By and by he was enabled to buy his bit outright. For there came a letter addressed to "The Pioneers of Perfection City" and containing a draft for five hundred dollars "for the hire of one horse" from an ever grateful friend. And Brother Dummy was given this money by the united wish of Olive, Ezra, Brother Green, and Uncle David, the last of the Pioneers, because, as they said, he was the only one who didn't know why it had been sent, and he was the only one who had not suffered through that episode that had so nearly wrecked their lives.

On a cold winter's day, when the snow lay in patches on the black prairie, Olive and her husband and Uncle David set out from Perfection City. She was pale and thin, and looked very ill as she stood leaning against the door-way of her dismantled home.

"I wish I could feel sorry at leaving the prairie, but I can't. I never want to see Perfection City again, but I'm sorry for my little home, and I would like to see my garden blossom again." So spoke Olive to Uncle David, standing beside her with shawls on his arm.

"Wal, now," replied he sadly, "we came here full o' the notion o' teachin' folks things, but it 'pears like as if it wasn't so much other folks out here as needed teachin' as jes' our own selves. We hev hed a hard lesson to learn, Ollie, my little gal, but I reckon we've pretty well learned it by now. It mos' likely comes to the same thing, on'y it's a sight more comfortin' to human pride to set up as a teacher than to sit down as a learner. We was as certain as anything we had a bran' new truth to teach to the world, an' we was goin' to show 'em how they'd been doin' wrong in everything 'fore we come to set 'em right. We was jes' bustin' with pride and vanity, that's what we was. We had foun' a new road to Kingdom Come, we had. 'Twasn't no road at all, on'y a coon track leadin' into a swamp. Guess we'll foller the road other folks has trod before, an' if we can fill up a slough or help anyone over the rough bits as is scattered plentiful all the way, that'll do for us. Ain't that your 'pinion, Ezry?"

"Yes, Uncle, we made a mistake. We thought

the great thing to do was to reform the ways of the world. We forgot that the human heart needed reforming first of all," said Ezra, looking sadly at his poor wan-cheeked little wife.

"And if the heart is right it doesn't matter about the rest, does it, dear?" said Olive, looking timidly at him.

He was sad and down-hearted and the eager enthusiasm was gone out of his manner. Ezra was much older-looking than he should have been, if life be reckoned by solar time alone. He had been aged by a lapse of mental time and suffering of which the almanac can take no heed. His wife saw and understood how he was, at this moment, realizing the downfall of his young hopes and beliefs, that was why he gazed so sadly across the desolate fields.

"We take nothing away with us except sad experience," he said as he lifted her into the waggon and drove off.

"And our love, dear, which nothing can ever destroy," she whispered, pressing his hand.

He stooped and kissed her. There were tears in his eyes. But they made a mistake. They took something else with them. Something that came tearing over the prairie with tongue out and tail stiff-stretched and nose to the ground—Diana, who had been turned over to Napoleon Pompey to have and to hold, but he could not hold her when she saw the waggon going off, therefore he could not have her. She caught them up when they were two miles off, and Olive let the dog clamber all over her, regardless of wet paws, and lick her face, so delighted were they to meet again.

THE END.

www.ingramcontent.com/pod-product-compliance
Lightning Source LLC
Chambersburg PA
CBHW030811230426
43667CB00008B/1167